A Bicentennial History
of
GREEN TOWNSHIP

Uncovering a Jewel in the Crown of the Queen City
1809–2009

Joe Flickinger

HERITAGE BOOKS
2011

HERITAGE BOOKS
AN IMPRINT OF HERITAGE BOOKS, INC.

Books, CDs, and more—Worldwide

For our listing of thousands of titles see our website
at
www.HeritageBooks.com

Published 2011 by
HERITAGE BOOKS, INC.
Publishing Division
100 Railroad Ave. #104
Westminster, Maryland 21157

Copyright © 2011 Joe Flickinger

Cover photo: Bridgetown Hotel
courtesy of the Wegman/Miller families

All rights reserved. No part of this book may be reproduced or transmitted in any form or by any means, electronic or mechanical, including photocopying, recording or by any information storage and retrieval system without written permission from the author, except for the inclusion of brief quotations in a review.

International Standard Book Numbers
Paperbound: 978-0-7884-5309-0
Clothbound: 978-0-7884-8745-3

Dedication

This book is dedicated to my wife and daughter. Your love and devotion to me and my pursuits has never wavered. Thank you for the support you gave me throughout the writing of this book.

Table of Contents

List of Illustrations...vii

Foreword...ix

Acknowledgements...xi

Introduction ...xiii

CHAPTER 1: The Early Days...1

CHAPTER 2: Early Life...18

CHAPTER 3: Township Communities are born...28

CHAPTER 4: The 20th Century and the Changes it brought...51

CHAPTER 5: Post-War Growth: Farms give way to subdivisions...77

CHAPTER 6: Looking ahead to 200 more years...95

Appendix...105-106

Bibliography...108-110

Index...112

List of Illustrations

1. John Cleves Symmes Sign
2. Schiable Creek
3. General Nathaniel Greene
4. Kuliga Park Sign
5. Dunn Cabin
6. Bailing Hay
7. Green Township Hotel
8. 1881 Map
9. Train Trestle
10. Receiving Vault
11. Dent Drive-In
12. Dent Schoolhouse
13. Aerial View of Mack
14. Monfort Heights Sign
15. C & W RR Crossing Glenmore
16. C & W Crossing Today
17. Seven Mile House
18. Harvest Home Fair
19. Wheat Wagon
20. C & W Engine #2
21. Population Chart
22. Frank Airport Opening
23. Hangar Today
24. 1st German Protestant Church
25. Ebenezer Methodist Church
26. St. James Church
27. St. Aloysius Church
28. Green Township Cemetery
29. Receiving Vault
30. Bridgetown Cemetery
31. Mack Firehouse
32. Anti-Thieving Badge
33. Dent School
34. Bridgetown School
35. Race Road in 1920's
36. Oak Hills High School
37. Bridgetown Finer Meats
38. Future Site of Mercy Hospital
39. German Heritage Museum
40. Good Samaritan Hospital
41. Neidhard Minges

Foreword

Green Township, located in western Hamilton County, celebrated its 200th birthday in 2009 – its Bicentennial. Green Township today looks a lot different than it did in the 1800s. Where you see houses, subdivisions, offices, and stores today you would have seen forests, farm fields, and farmhouses in those days.

In Joe Flickinger's *A Bicentennial History of Green Township: Uncovering a Jewel in* the *Crown of the Queen City*, you will learn about the development and growth of the township. Beginning with its days as a Shawnee hunting ground, to its early settlement by hunters and trappers, to the farming days of the nineteenth century to the transformation to a series of suburban communities in the twentieth century. Today the township has one of the largest township populations in the state of Ohio.

Kuliga Park is one of the township's principal parks – what does Kuliga mean? How did the Green Township communities, Dent and Mack, get their unique names? Why is the township called "Green" Township? Joe's fascinating book will shed light on these and many more interesting aspects of Green Township's history.

The Green Township Historical Association was proud to assist Joe in this effort. He is a Green Township native, teaches history in a local school district and is a member of the Green Township Historical Association. *A Bicentennial History of Green Township: Uncovering a Jewel in the Crown of the Queen City* is one of only a few histories of the township ever published. Enjoy reading about the Green Township story.

Paul J. Ruffing
Green Township Historical Association

Acknowledgements

I would like to thank The Green Township Historical Association and its President, Paul Ruffing, for their help and support in this endeavor. Their help and seemingly unending archives helped me tremendously in completing this book. To everyone who submitted pictures and anecdotes, thank you as well. To my grandparents, Dorothy Warren and John and Margaret Flickinger, without your support and wisdom I would have never have tried to write, much less considered researching a topic as big as this book. To my dad, Bill Flickinger, who passed his love of history to me and my mom, Nancy Flickinger, who passed her tenacity and love of writing, I want to thank you as well. To all my past teachers, instructors, and professors who encouraged me in some way, shape or form, thank you as well. Finally to the people of Green Township; may the next 200 years be as bright and cheerful as the last 200 years have been.

Introduction

"Eighty-eight miles per hour!" This famous line from the movie *Back to the Future* was uttered by old Doc Brown when the time machine created from his converted DeLorean transported him to a different era without harm to man or animal. Many people who are now in their 30's and 40's look back on that movie because they identified with characters, or with one particular character, from that movie. The hip teen who found himself thrust into his hometown in 1955 instead of 1985 was one of my favorite movie characters as well. Besides being an entertaining movie, it set the stage for my thoughts in regards to the history of the area where I lived: Green Township.

As I grew older, I began to wonder about the area in which I lived. I knew that changes were occurring quickly in Green Township. Roads which once saw light traffic were now clogged with traffic backups from the families living in expanding subdivisions. Once open fields that bordered our school were now being bulldozed over, graded, and built out with offices and homes. I fondly remember feeding horses carrots and apples during class in 1st grade at the farm which bordered my elementary school, Oakdale. The Brockhoff Farm existed for generations of students and township residents. I knew it as a place that boarded horses. I happily think back to watching these magnificent animals running along free on their property which shared a school on one side, and busy Bridgetown Road on the other. I guess looking back I should have thought it inevitable that at some point a developer would eye the property and give the right price for the land to be developed. Today this land is light office space and condos.

But, as many pieces of property like this farm succumbed to development, I wondered what it would be like to speed down one of the streets at eighty-eight mph in a DeLorean, and go back 200 years to meet Jacob Johnson, one of the characters in Green Township History. Would he be interested in what I had to say about what would become of the heavily wooded area he helped clear for settlement? Would Samuel Lewis be interested in hearing how education has changed in the township since he left the area as a teacher to become the first Superintendent of Ohio's Public Schools? Would Charles Reemelin be delighted to know that the area he renamed for the physical nature of the area would still be known as Dent in the 21st century? Would the original Catholic settlers who established St. James in White Oak be intrigued by the explosion of Catholic churches and schools in the area in the 20th century? Would Enoch Carson be surprised that his little harvest celebration continues to be a yearly celebration enjoyed by young and old alike? How interesting would it be to rumble down Bridgetown Road in the DeLorean and see up close and personal the second St. Aloysius Church building loom over the fields, and the Bridgetown Saloon serving up Herancourt Beer? I would love to see that, and knowing what I know now about Green Township history, this area would have been just as interesting to live in before the growth and changes that are taking place now.

  I hope you find this trip through 200 years of history fun and entertaining. I know I really enjoyed writing about it. No other major comprehensive history of the area has been written, and while it was a daunting task writing the book, it was truly a labor of love.

  Green Township has developed into more than just a place to grow food or raise animals. It has emerged as a vibrant place for people to live. It may have taken 200 years to reach over 60,000 residents but when word spread about this area, like the narrator said in *Field of Dreams,* "If you build it, people will come." In 200 years, people have affirmed the value of life in this beautiful community. I hope you are able to sit with family members who are lifelong residents of Green Township and reminisce about the many changes witnessed over the years. Perhaps you can tell your children and grandchildren about the way this community used to look. The Green Township of today wouldn't exist without the sacrifice of those before us. The past 200 years are gone. Join in with me as I look into the future and celebrate Green Township as one of the jewels in the crown of the Queen City.

Chapter One:
The Early Days

Green Township and its encompassing communities are well known to their inhabitants, but not as well known to many native Cincinnatians unfamiliar with the western side of Cincinnati. The "Westside" as it is known, draws the ire of many "outsiders" because of its unique closeness and its small town feel within 10 miles of a major Midwestern city. Many outsiders venture into the "Westside" to visit friends and relatives, or attend community events, and emerge surprised and befuddled by crazy locations of streets, neighborhoods, and community institutions. The Green Township of today does not even come close to the Green Township of pioneer days when Native Americans labeled this area "kuliga". The Green Township of pioneer days was a frontier land, far removed from the small little settlement known to many as Losantiville; Green Township was dotted with beautiful trickling streams abundant with many types of fish and other wildlife such as deer, rabbits, and the occasional bear or two. The Green Township of the late 1700's also had lush, thick forests, making travel through the area by wagon almost impossible unless old Native Americans trails were followed. Even then, travel on foot or horseback was an absolute necessity, as many of these old trails were less than 5 feet wide, making settlement in the area very, very slow.

       In order to understand the slow settlement of Green Township one must understand many of the obstacles placed in the way of the early settlers to the area. The Native Americans in the area, the Shawnee, were very hostile towards white settlement in the land north of the Ohio due to their labeling of the Ohio Country as their own "sacred hunting ground". At first, many white hunters and trappers navigated their way through the area and made positive contact with the Shawnee and other tribes living in the Ohio Country.

These hunters and trappers hunted for a few months, bartered and traded with the local tribes, and moved on in short order. This contact occurred until the end of the American Revolution, when the Proclamation of 1763 was repealed, and settlement opened to just about anyone who wished to move to the newly opened "wild west". The Proclamation of 1763 forbade any further settlement into the Ohio territory by British subjects, but this didn't stop some. Many individuals were lured to this new "wild west" by the idea of making a fresh start, a new beginning where they could make a substantial change in their life. The Ohio territory became a bastion for those seeking a new beginning. Despite the Proclamation of 1763, settlement increased, with many individuals choosing the Ohio Valley as an excellent place to start over. Many of these settlers were native Virginians, choosing to stay Virginians by settling in the Ohio Valley. Virginia owned a large chunk of the Ohio Territory, and many of the Virginians who moved here did so with the idea that many of the British Royal agents who oversaw Virginia were not going to see the movement as anything to pay attention to, due to the large distance between the main urban areas of Virginia proper and the Ohio territory.

  During the American Revolution, the Ohio Territory became an area of contention for both colonists and Native Americans. Some settlers saw the area as a bastion of opportunity that was theirs for the taking. Native Americans became disenfranchised by the breaking of the Proclamation of 1763 by the American Colonists. Soon the Native Americans became very sympathetic towards the British cause. Many Native Americans saw the vast, lush wilderness that they considered their sacred hunting ground being destroyed by the methods used by the new eastern transplants to establish their homes. Colonists stripped the land, with little to no regard for the environment around them.

Trees that were hundreds of years old were quickly disappearing in favor of open fields. By the end of the American Revolution, Green Township was still an unabashed wilderness, but things were about to change. While the founding fathers were meeting back east, a few pioneers were making their way to the Ohio Territory by way of the Cumberland Gap and the newly organized territory of Kentucky. Word began to trickle east about the beauty and abundance of the Ohio Country. One of those individuals who heard of the potential for growth and profit was a man named Benjamin Stites. Stites made several forays into the area, and decided to enlist the help of others in his quest to settle and profit from this "wild west".

An important individual to the history of Green Township who was synonymous with the settlement of Cincinnati was John Cleves Symmes. Symmes was a delegate to the Continental Congress and judge from New Jersey in 1788 when he acquired over 311,000 acres from Congress.[1] In November of that year, Stites and a small group of settlers made their way down the Ohio River on flatboats and settled in what are today the eastern suburbs of Cincinnati. Stites and his settlers named their settlement Columbia. In December of that year, Robert Patterson and Mathias Denman led a second group of settlers down the Ohio River and landed at what is now the Public Landing area of the riverfront of Cincinnati. They named their tiny settlement Losantiville. In 1789, Symmes himself made his way down the river with a third group of settlers and landed

---

[1] Iola Silberstein, <u>Cincinnati, Then and Now</u>, (Cincinnati, League of Women Voters, 1982) 10.

west of the Losantiville site, and Symmes named his settlement North Bend, for the steep northern bend the river takes. [2]

Settlement was slow in the territory known as the Northwest Territory, due in part to the hostile actions taken by the native tribes in the area. In 1790, due to increasing fears of the Shawnee tribes, the United States Army was directed by President George Washington to erect a fort for the protection of US citizens settling the area. Fort Washington was built to be able to hold over 200 troops and be a warning to all native tribes considering attacks. Due to the presence of the fort, settlement remained along the riverfront. Settlement would remain there after a pioneer outpost called Fort Dunlap (in what would later be named Colerain Township) was attacked near the Great Miami River in January 1791. Shawnee forces led by Simon Girty numbering over 300 surrounded and laid siege to the fort which was manned by 18 federal regulars and an officer from Ft. Washington.[3] After reinforcements arrived from Fort Washington and scared off the invaders, settlement almost stopped in what would become neighboring Green Township.

Green Township would be a hunter's paradise today if left untouched by the eventual development throughout the years. But once the Indians were banished from Ohio with the signing of the Treaty of Greenville in 1795, the Green Township the hunters, trappers and Natives knew would change forever. The first known permanent settler in Green Township was James Goudy, who hiked his way into the area around 1802.[4] Goudy, a Pennsylvania hunter, came to Green

---

[2] Silberstein, 9-10
[3] Edwin Kramb, Buckeye Battlefields,(Sprinboro Ohio,Valhalla Press)
[4] Hale, Harry, Kuliga, The Pretty Land, (Western Hills Press) 3

Historical Marker located in the Congress Green Cemetery where the grave of John Cleves Symmes and his family lie. This cemetery is next to the William Henry Harrison Presidential Tomb, located in nearby North Bend, Ohio. Symmes and Harrison played major roles in the early sale of Green Township lands. (Photo by Joe Flickinger)

Township with his sister, Rebecca, and his younger brother, Hugh. He was described as the "most massive and strongest man" in the Green Township woods. He settled in the NW corner of Section 8 of the township. This area today is considered to be a part of the Cincinnati neighborhood of Westwood. Once he had hewn his cabin he became the first permanent resident of Green Township. The second family to make their way to the township was the Johnson family, led by Jacob Johnson in late 1802 to early 1803. He built his cabin on the NW corner of section 9 of the township, now a part of the city of Cheviot. He was given most of the western half of section 9 by John Cleves Symmes in 1805 for his help in cutting an early road from the Mill Creek to present day Harrison Ohio. This road today is known as Harrison Ave. Johnson was also one of the settlers that made their way down the Ohio River with Symmes as one of the original inhabitants of North Bend. Like Goudy, he was also described as a massive man, being "massively stout". The cabins of these men were 12 x 15 feet, having been built using round buckeye logs, utilizing clapboard roofs and clapboard doors. Both cabins had fireplaces with stick and mud chimneys. They also had the advantage of the first natural indoor refrigeration system, by using a four foot hole dug in the middle of the cabin floor which was covered up. It was called the "potato hole" and would keep food fresh and cool for days. These two families were the only residents of Green Township until 1804.

  In 1805, a handful of individuals made the trek up the western hills surrounding Cincinnati and settled in Green Township. Many of these frontier farms remained isolated until little towns and villages began to spring up to host the businesses that would service the coming explosion of farms in the area.

  Before Green Township was able to support permanent settlers, the Congress of the United States

This picture shows the uncovered portion of Schaible Creek which follows Westbourne Drive and empties into Muddy Creek. A typical trapper from Green Township in the early 1800's would have hacked their way through brush and wilderness just like this. (Photo by Joe Flickinger)

had set up rules for governing and dividing what was being called the public domain. The Land Ordinance of 1785 created the guidelines for the shape and character of what would be called Green Township. According to the Land Ordinance, townships were to be divided into six mile square townships created by lines running north and south and intersecting at right angles with east/west lines. Townships were to be arranged in north/south rows called ranges. Most townships were to be subdivided into 36 one mile square sections. Each range, township and section was to be numbered in a regular, consistent sequence. [5]

    As the Symmes purchase was first settled in 1788, the area was split into 3 distinct townships: Columbia, Losantiville, and Miami. These townships were three huge areas encompassing almost all of what is now modern Hamilton County. These three townships were formed from the three original settlements of the Symmes Purchase. These three areas were: Columbia, settled by Benjamin Stites in November 1788;, Losantiville, settled in late December 1788, and North Bend, established by John Cleves Symmes in 1789. The Green Township we know of today had its roots in portions of the original Miami and Losantiville townships. Losantiville Township became known as Cincinnati Township after the Governor of the Northwest Territory, Arthur St. Claire, visited Losantiville and renamed it Cincinnati. Another reason for St. Claire's visit was the establishment of a county, which they named Hamilton, in honor of the current Treasury Secretary and Revolutionary War hero, Alexander Hamilton. In 1795, South Bend Township was established to accommodate the brand new settlement close to what is now Anderson Ferry, by Timothy Symmes, who was the only full brother

---

[5] Dr. George Knepper, The Official Ohio Lands Book (Columbus Ohio, Auditor of the State of Ohio Publication, 2002) 13-16

of John Cleves Symmes. North Bend was touted by John Cleves Symmes as the future home of the metropolis of the purchase area, because of its central location. This idea was supported by a detachment of 21 Federal Troops stationed there for a short time before the establishment of Fort Washington. Unfortunately, the area grew undesirable when flood waters forced the abandonment of the settlement to higher ground until the waters subsided. Much of the Symmes Purchase area remained loosely organized, remaining huge townships while most of the attention for settlement was given to Cincinnati after the establishment of Ft. Washington. South Bend Township included all of Delhi Township and most of Green Township. Small sections of today's northern Green Township were claimed by Colerain Township, which was formed in 1794. These civic divisions changed in 1803 when Ohio was admitted to the United States as the 17th State. This is when sources indicate that Hamilton County began to shrink, as many newer counties were formed from Hamilton County. Among these newer counties included Butler and Warren counties to the north, and Clermont County to the east. Hamilton County, came very close to the shape it is today. From this point, surveyors began carving up Hamilton County into the various different townships as outlined in the Land Ordinance of 1785. Green Township became labeled within the Symmes Purchase as Fractional Range 2, Township 2. It is the only township created in the Symmes Purchase which was a complete 36 square miles. The accepted date of creation for Green Township is 1809. While no actual documentation is known to have survived, a modern source indicates a possible clue to the beginning of the township. The state law stipulated that once a suitable amount of men wanted to establish a government, the County Constable must call a meeting and he helps choose a chairman of the meeting. He was given orders to arrest anyone who disturbed the meeting. Fifteen male taxpayers had to be present, and they in turn elected officials by secret ballot. These officials consisted of three or more trustees, two overseers of the poor, three fenceviewers, two appraisers of houses, one lister of property and a number of supervisors of land. In those days, holding office wasn't considered an honor. After being elected to office, anyone refusing was fined $5. By 1831 it was reduced to a fine of $2. After 1850, the offices paid too much to be refused.[6] While no complete list of past Green Township trustees is known to exist, the first members of the South Bend township, which much of Green Township is known to have originated from, is known. The first township clerk was William Powell, the first constable was James Thatcher, the first overseers of the poor were William Powell and Robert Goudy, the first supervisor of highways was Usual Bates, and the first viewers of enclosures were David Edgar, James Goudy, Edward Cowan.[7]

Today, the Green Township slate of elected officials has been reduced to 3 township trustees, and a fiscal officer. They all run for office using modern political campaigns, and are voted on by all township residents who are 18 years old and registered to vote. Any other positions within township administration are voted upon by the trustees, and many of the jobs, including the police and fire departments, use modern civil service examinations to produce the best and brightest candidates for possible approval by the township trustees.[8]

---

[6] Henry Scully ed, <u>Remember When…Monfort Heights</u> (Cincinnati Ohio, Monfort Heights Civic Association, 1977) 19

[7] Henry and Kate Ford, <u>History of Hamilton County Ohio</u>, (Cleveland Ohio, L.A. Williams Publishers, 1881) 294

[8] Green Township Webpage, (updated 11/2010, accessed 6/2010) http://www.greentwp.org

The name Green Township is also something that is easily confused today. Many individuals assume that the name is to describe the area as it was found by the settlers. While that would be a good assumption, the actual origin of the name of the township is the misnomer it is today. The township was named after Nathaniel Greene, a famous General in the American Revolution. He was one of George Washington's most trusted advisors, and was quite a notable strategist and advisor for the General. Throughout the years, the "e" at the end of the name was dropped and for most the meaning has changed to the current place name.[9] The only remembrance easily visible today is the Nathaniel Greene Lodge built by the township in the late 1990's.

Another problem encountered by early Green Township was its location within the Symmes purchase. According to the rules set out by the Northwest Territory, land was set aside for educational purposes. This came to fruition as a college township. A college township was land that was to be set aside for the exclusive use and establishment of a college or university. Green Township was one of the choices by Symmes to be a college township. Through many land deals he had already sold parts of the "college" townships he was considering to private individuals. Mill Creek Township, and Springfield Township were to be considered first, but parts of those townships were sold off, in part because he was holding back Green Township for himself. Symmes then tried to push what would become Green Township as the choice for a college, but the Federal Government sent a scouting committee to examine the land in 1800. The committee sent a recommendation for rejection of Green Township because it was "too rough for farming, and too wild for civilized life."[10] What they probably did

---

[9]Charles Reemelin, <u>Historical Sketch of Greene Township</u>, (Cincinnati Ohio, Robert Clarke Publishers, 1882) 9
[10] Reemelin, 21

General Nathaniel Greene, Revolutionary War hero, after whom the township is named (Painting by Charles Wilson Peale)

was made it to the edge of Green Township, realized they were at the edge of the known world and couldn't fathom a college, much less anything civilized at all, taking place in such a deep and dark wooded area that was Green Township in 1800. Symmes also lost a court hearing in Pennsylvania Circuit Court where part of his holdings in Green Township were given to one of his partners, Elias Boudinot. This action solidified the Federal Government's rejection of Green Township as the college township in the Symmes Purchase. The college township actually ended up being placed outside of the Symmes Purchase and Hamilton County completely. This college town was Oxford, Ohio which is located in Butler County, which currently hosts Miami University.[11]

Kuliga: Pretty Land or Pretty Hand?

Native American Shawnee who lived in the area during the frontier times were quoted by the early settlers, including the Johnsons and later the Reemelins, as calling the area later known as Green Township, "Kuliga". According to Harry J. Hale, the word Kuliga is translated as meaning "Pretty Land". Since his research was published by the Western Hills Press in 1949, this has been the translation that has been accepted by many living in the township. In 1976 a new 30 acre park was opened on Bridgetown Road, which was named Kuliga. Many residents thought the park was given the name to describe its beauty. Or so it was thought. In 1977 a rebuttal was published in the Western Hills Press by local historian Marjorie Burress. She describes a speech made by Charles Reemelin at the 1882 Harvest Home Festival on the subject of the early days of the township.

---

[11] Reemelin, 21

In this speech, Burress described how Reemelin described the name Ku-li-ga as being Shawnee for "Pretty Hand". It was meant to describe the approach along Taylor's Creek from the Great Miami River, where the small tributaries that branched off of Taylor's Creek resembled the fingers from an outstretched hand.[12] Even today, as current scholarship moves forward, the mystery of the real meaning of the Shawnee word Kuliga rages on. According to Michael McCafferty, an Algonquian and Uto-Aztecan linguist in Indiana University's Department of Second Language Studies, Kuliga as written does not have any meaning in the Shawnee language.[13] Ms. Burress used as an example the word Ki-le-chi from the Shawnee dictionary in the back of the best selling novel *The Frontiersman* as the actual word that Reemelin was supposed to have meant to use.[14] Mr. McCafferty said that ""Ki-Leh-Chi" is an excellent amateur phonetic representation of Shawnee "Your Finger", /ki-/ 'your' + /-leci/'finger': /kileci/, where /c/ is "ch". But "-liga" could be a commendable, albeit misheard, Shawnee /-leca/ 'hand'. Algonquian /i/ and /e/ were commonly confused by English (and French) speakers, so the first vowel of "-liga" is not a problem." McCafferty goes on to say that "'The "-g-" would be what he would term an "alphabet G". In other words, early historic English speakers often wrote letters just like they sounded in the recited English alphabet. Here, in "Kuliga," it appears that the English speaker heard the sound /j/, written G as in "Germany," for /c/, commonly written "ch" in English. The final vowel, "-a" is somewhat problematic, since early historic English speakers often wrote "a" for Algonquian /i/. But the final "-a" could just as well represent a real /a/. That was also a

---

[12] Marjorie Burress, "What does Kuliga Really Mean?" Western Hills Press, 1977
[13] Michael McCafferty, email interview, 6/16/2008
[14] Allan W. Eckert, <u>The Frontiersman,</u> (Asland Kentucky, Jesse Stuart Foundation Publishers, 2001) 614

No matter what the word Kuliga actually was meant to describe, most township residents associate the name with the busy township park located on Bridgetown Road, which was established in 1976. (Photo Courtesy Green Township Historical Asscoation)

historical possibility for these English speakers. In the first case, you get "finger"; in the second case, you'd get "hand". Since the name was translated "XXX-hand," this final "-a" of "Kuliga" probably stands for /a/. Now, what "Ku-"means is downright opaque. If it is a miscopied "Ki-," which is not out of the question in terms of common historical miscopied letters, then the name means "Your-Hand".'[15]

    No matter which word was actually spoken to the Johnson's and later told to Charles Reemelin, the word does add a bit of color to this already beautiful area of Ohio. Beautiful Land or Hand, it still describes a land that is unique to the already different landscape of the soon to be blooming city that would become Cincinnati.

---

[15] Michael McCafferty, email interview, 6/16/2008

Chapter Two:
Early Life

As mentioned before, the Green Township of today is very different from the Green Township of yesterday. In today's world of cell phones, computers, and HDTV, the common 21st century individual would find the frontier life of the Goudy's and Johnson's very hard indeed. Most would find it very quiet, and in the case of Green Township, very lonely. Most of these individuals had to begin fresh wherever they went. Literally, they would have to clear the land, and at the same time finish a permanent dwelling as quickly as possible. Without a permanent dwelling, life in Green Township was next to impossible.

When settlers first arrived, the first accomplishment was the establishment of shelter. Since most of the individuals who made their way to Green Township first were the men, a quick lean-to was the cheap and quick solution to the shelter issue. Many families would later join the men after a more permanent shelter was underway or finished. Many of these early cabins were neither fancy nor comfortable. As described earlier, the Goudy's and Johnson's cabins were not very big. Many families lived, slept, and ate in the same room. Children ran around all day never putting on a pair of shoes in the spring, summer, and fall. Many of the farmers spent a majority of their first year clearing the land for use as fields to grow their crops. Next was the establishment of a reliable water supply. Many of the township's creeks and streams provided the water necessary to grow the crops as well as quench the thirst of the growing township. One such example of establishing a farm close to a major creek was the Schaible family. Their 28 acre farm was established along today's Westbourne Drive between Muddy Creek and Werk Road. Much of our knowledge about the workings of a frontier farm is from the writings of both

Theresa and Charles Schaible. They wrote plenty about the Muddy Creek, indicating the importance it played in the family's everyday life. They wrote that not only were the creeks and streams a vital lifeline for health and survival, they were a guide used to find ones way into town, as a pathway to church, as a compass to school, and also a route to finding the neighbors. Quite a large amount of Muddy Creek and it's tributary creeks like Schaible Creek today has been covered over and made into a sewer culvert. The covered section runs from Werk Rd. along Glenway, across Lawrence Rd. to Bridgetown Rd., and across the low points of Ruebel Place, Bridgetown Cemetery, Weirman Ave. and Church Lane. It then crosses Harrison Ave. passing behind the current Stacey's Place Tavern, under School Section and into the City of Cheviot. One could only imagine the Schaible's using the creek as a guide to the then town of Cheviot, or to a neighbor's farm in Bridgetown. Theresa Schiable also wrote about using the creek as a guide to get to Ruebels Saloon in Bridgetown (the former Wagon Wheel Café) to get whiskey for her father to drink with the well water. She wrote how she was embarrassed to go there in her bare feet.[16] Today, they would be quite surprised at the changes in the modern world! Many of the farms in Green Township had the added bonus of rolling hills which would have made planting crops difficult. Many of these rolling hills made excellent pastures for horses, cows, pigs, and the occasional goat or sheep. In the flatter portions of the farms, the staple crops like potatoes and corn were grown. Often the seasons would dictate what would be grown. Throughout the growing season fruits like cherries, peaches, apples, and melons were grown and either sold immediately at one of the many markets in Cincinnati, were consumed by the family, or made into preserves. Vegetables like cabbage, onions,

---

[16] Theresa Schaible, <u>My Family</u>, Self Published Family History, 1945

The Dunn cabin, located at Shawnee Lookout Park, in Western Hamilton County. Built in 1795 in Elizabethtown Ohio, this cabin represented what many of the cabins in Green Township would have looked like during pioneer days. (Picture by Joe Flickinger)

tomatoes, and various varieties of corn were grown and also either used on the farm or sold at market. Often one trip per week would be organized in the early days into Cincinnati, due to the distance and roads into the city. Sometimes, the overabundance of certain crops would lead to their disposal in the city. Phillip Steinman III recounted in his book "Beechwood Flats" about often having to often dump excess crops like tomatoes into the Mill Creek because everyone had bought their fill. According to Steinman, even the ketchup factories wouldn't take the tomatoes, and since they had more than their fair share back on the farm, they would just dump them in the water![17] Often travel would be next to impossible due to the swampy conditions in the Mill Creek valley. A farmer would often return to Green Township with an empty wagon, for fear of getting stuck in the mud or wearing down horses for the arduous journey up the hills and back home. As a result, the settlement of Green Township remained slow, and as mentioned before, trips were organized on a weekly, or monthly basis, depending on Mother Nature's schedule, of course!

Rural Living takes shape

Much of the news was spread in the early times by communications between the neighbors. Without the aid of cell phones or computers, much of the instant messaging between friends was accomplished by a swift ride by horseback from neighbor to neighbor. Consequently, much of the news was old news when it reached the farmers of Green Township. The only events that were spread quickly were death or a birth. Often a member of the very large families would hop on the swiftest horse in order to inform the neighbors and

---

[17] Philip Steinman III, Beechwood Flats, (New York NY, Vantage Press, 1960) 17

Bailing hay on the farm in early Green Township. This was a familiar sight throughout the township. (Picture courtesy Green Township Historical Association)

friends of the big event. Often many of the neighbors were close by, since many of the farms and homesteads were small at 40 acres or less. As an added bonus, many of the people who lived in close proximity were not only neighbors, but family members as well. One such example was along the Werk Rd. area of Green Township, where various members of the Oliger/Neiheisel/Schaible family were not only neighbors, but family as well. Many of these houses and some of the rural character built into them are still evident in today's Green Township.

By the 1850 census, the United States was a burgeoning country, with major cities such as New York, Philadelphia, Baltimore, Pittsburgh, and Cincinnati ruling the countryside's they straddled. In 1848, a major revolution in an area of Europe known today as Germany sent a large influx of German settlers and refugees into the Cincinnati area.[18] The townships population nearly doubled from 1820, from 1,475, to 3,948 in 1850. From early on, the amount of farms and subsequent little hamlets began to multiply. Most of the little hamlets became names on a map from the increased population shift west. Add in the 48'ers and the subsequent German immigration, and you have a recipe for a stable almost steady flow of traffic to the outlying rural communities of Green Township. If one were to meet one of these individuals, one might find the individual German of Cincinnati would have met a certain stereotype set down by many native born Americans. Many Germans were described as having heavy beards, and wearing a different hat than other Americans. Many of these immigrants were highly thought of for their competence in business affairs and frugal natures, which gained the respect of immigrants and native born Americans all over Cincinnati.[19] This thrift and competence can be

---

[18] Don Heinrich Tolzmann, German Heritage Guide to the Greater Cincinnati Area (Milford Ohio, Little Miami Publishing, 2003) 13
[19] Tolzmann, 14

This photo shows the Green Township Hotel, a popular rest stop along Harrison Ave. Horses could be watered, food and drink could be consumed, and news could be spread about various happenings in the area. This building was located close to where North Bend Road dead-ends into Harrison Ave. (photo courtesy Green Township Historical Association)

frequently attributed in the way many of these rural farmers lived. Many were not overly wealthy but were simple, thrifty individuals who made the best out of what they could. Once one made their way to the Mill Creek at the base of what is now the Western Hills Viaduct, one did not see the sprawling neighborhoods associated with today's suburbs. One would see the wide open, fresh air of country living. Life would be very slow, and to some, very monotonous. But this way of life did have some perks. Many of these farmers made their way into Cincinnati to sell their goods in the many markets throughout the city's neighborhoods. Others loaded up their wagons and ventured into Price Hill or Clifton to sell their goods. Many farmers drove their cattle, pigs, and other livestock through the muddied roads into the city for the many slaughterhouses that made up a vital piece of the Cincinnati economy in the 1800's. Even though the population may have been small compared to Cincinnati, Green Township was a very necessary cog in the industrial machine that Cincinnati was developing into. Life was slow, but very rewarding.

   Often, the monotony of the daily grind was broken up by various activities. One such activity was the breaking of wild horses that had been delivered to the various farmers.[20] Another was the wayward traveling salesman who might be chased up the nearest tree by the family dog. Many families preferred bulldogs or Newfoundland's as the family pets due to their protective nature. These traveling salesmen would often bear needles, thread, and other various different sundry items that the farms would need but couldn't justify a day's journey into Cincinnati; they would put these items in a bag and make their way from farm to farm. One of the very telling facts about the nature of the families and farmers is that they would often invite the salesmen to

---

[20] Steinman, 20

eat with them after quelling the upset guard dogs that patrolled the early farms.[21] This tells the 21st century person of the goodwill and good nature of the pioneer farmers during the early days of our township. The farmers and subsequent communities were closely knit, and the families were even closer. Even though this rural way of life may have given way to suburban developments, the close ties that people feel towards Green Township still persist, and add a very real connection and pride to the area that many communities of today lack.

---

[21] Steinman, 21-22

Chapter Three:
Township Communities are born

The Green Township of the 1820's to the early 1920's was a growing community, albeit at a snail's pace compared to today. Life moved slowly, and many of the distinct communities sprang up from the frontier as a place where the farmers could visit to get supplies from the shops and vendors who set up businesses to sell their wares in these new rural hamlets. These communities, many with no real borders, make up the confusing place names that confuse many "outsiders" to the Westside today.

Life in these areas was slow, and it seemed the outside world passed by these areas of Cincinnati without a second thought. Word was slow to reach these areas of the election of William Henry Harrsion from nearby North Bend as the 9th President, and then his subsequent death a month after taking office.

While issues and problems began to rise and create tensions in the country over the issue of slavery, life pushed on without much thought or debate on the issue. Why should it? Slavery was never allowed in the old Northwest Territory. Ohio was admitted as a free state in 1803. The farmers and ranchers in these hamlets were hard workers who toiled on the land and reaped the benefits. As the Civil War raged on, various sons, brothers, and fathers went off to war; some returned changed by the experience. They were a little more hardened, a little quieter and subdued than before they left. Some of these individuals never made it home alive; their families grieved, but life moved on- it had to, there was work to do. Green Township sent some of its sons and fathers to far away places and events like the Mexican War, the Boxer Rebellion, the Spanish American War, and the Great War, WWI. But while all of these major world events were raging, life in Green Township would stay pretty much the same. These people were tied to the land, and as a result, the seasons. Spring brought

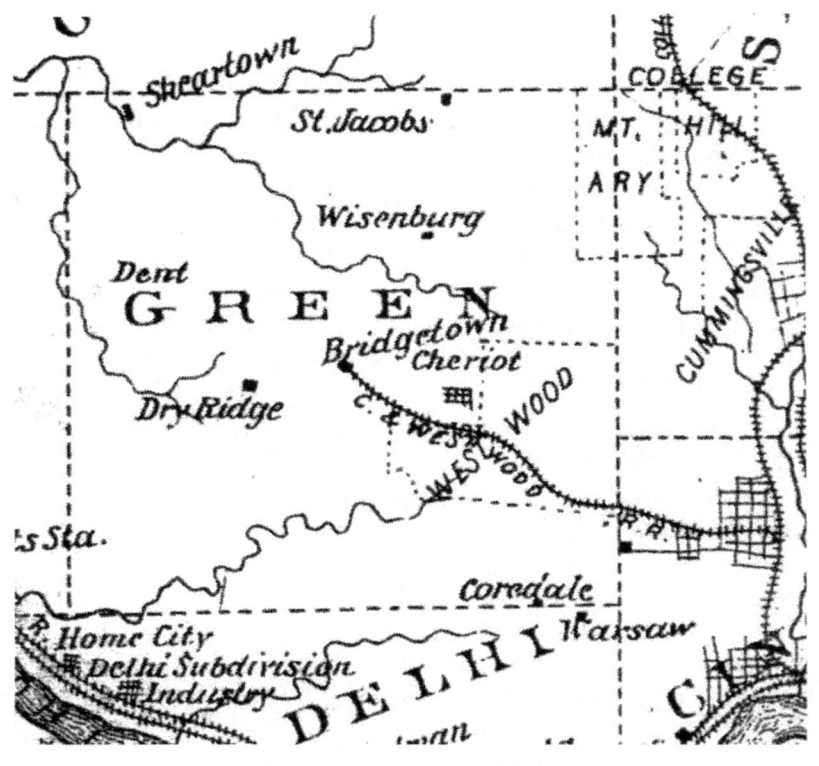

1881 Map of Green Township. Notice Westwood and Mt Airy are already delineating themselves from rural Green Township. Dry Ridge would be today's Mack. Wisenburg would be today's Monfort Heights, St. Jacobs is today's White Oak, and Sheartown is today's Taylor Creek. (Map Courtesy Green Township Historical Association)

the tilling and planting. Summer brought the raising of the crops and the first small harvests. Fall brought the major harvests, and preparations for winter. Winter saw life slowed to a crawl. With the breaking of winter and transition into spring, the cycle started over again. In the midst of all this, communities gained a unique character all their own. While they each had different origins and beginnings, they all have one thing in common: they are all Green Township communities.

<u>Bridgetown</u>

Bridgetown is located in the central portion of the township. The epicenter of this hamlet is the confluence of Race Rd, Bridgetown Rd, and Glenway Ave. This hamlets name is one of the most well known Green Township settlements to Cincinnatians. There have been many myths about the origin of the name Bridgetown. Many "outsiders" assume that the name Bridgetown comes from some sort of bridge that allowed passage over a waterway, and alludes to the town that sprung up around this bridge. Those outsiders are wrong. Even though the aforementioned branch of the Muddy Creek passed right through the middle of Bridgetown, this is not the case. Many "natives" believe that the name comes from the old C & O Railroad trestle that crossed the major intersection of Bridgetown Rd, Race Rd, and Glenway Ave. Those natives would be wrong as well. The actual origin of the name is tied to an early family that moved here from the Bridgeton New Jersey area. This family's name was the Fithian family, who came to this area around 1820 and established a saw mill. The train trestle wasn't built until the early 1900's, and in the *Pioneer Annals of Green Township*,[22] the area is referred to as Bridgeton, giving additional evidence to the Fithian

---

[22] Reese P. Kendall, MD, <u>Pioneer Annals of Green Township</u>, (San Jose California, 1905)

The Bridgetown train trestle, which crossed over the intersection of Bridgetown, Glenway, and Race Roads, as seen in 1984 shortly before it was removed. (Photo Courtesy of the Green Township Historical Association)

family and their influence on the area. The Bridgetown area is also referred to by this name as early as 1847 on a county map. Like many of the areas of Green Township, Bridgetown has no real borders, and overlaps with many other areas including Dent, Mack, and Monfort Heights.

One of the oldest buildings which was recently demolished to make way for a widened intersection was the Wagon Wheel Café, which has been a tavern or saloon since the mid-1800's, and it was acquired by the Christian Ruebel family, at the intersection of Race, Glenway, and Bridgetown roads. They named it the Bridgetown Hotel and Saloon. It was later operated by LJ Andawan as the "First and Last Chance Saloon". It was a major landmark in the Green Township area. It was one of many stops that the local farmers made while driving their cattle, pigs, and other livestock and crops to Cincinnati for sale at the many farmers markets or slaughterhouses located within the city limits. In later years, many current residents know it by the name the Wagon Wheel Café. Its neon sign shone brightly in the night sky at the busy intersection, guiding the way for many individuals throughout the late 1950's though the early 2000's.

Yet another old building still in existence today is the receiving vault in the Bridgetown Cemetery. This building, which resembles a small chapel, was designed and built by local stone mason Phillip Steinman I in 1876, and was dedicated in 1877.[23] It was built with the express purpose of holding bodies until the ground thawed in the winter, or if the body needed a place to be kept until the burial. Today, it is used as a storage facility for tools and equipment for the cemetery. Walking through the original portion of the cemetery gives one the feel and character that made up frontier Bridgetown. Many of the names on the headstones

---

[23] Steinman, 11

Receiving vault located in the oldest portion of the Bridgetown Cemetery. Dedicated in 1877, this building harkens back to a much simpler time in Bridgetown's history. (Photo by Joe Flickinger)

represent the hardworking farmers and ranchers that toiled the land, traveled the macadam roads, and enjoyed the peaceful country life. One can shut out the cars, planes, and other loud noises of the 21st century and if you listen hard enough, you can hear the whispers of the kids at play in the corn fields; the blast of a shotgun taking aim at rabbits or squirrels; or the sounds of the many farm animals that made Bridgetown the typical rural American community.

    The Bridgetown of today is considered a "bedroom community", many of the homes that were built in the 1950's are numerous and where people live; yet work elsewhere. The Bridgetown of today is a vast expanse of subdivisions, traffic, restaurants and a mixture of chain stores and small independent shops. Contrast that with the 1800's, when you might be lucky to see some people other than your family once a day! In the1800's one might see more livestock than people traveling the roads. Today, one might sit in traffic at lights and deal with traffic jams with line after line of cars!

<u>Dent</u>

    The community of Dent was established along Harrison Pike at the intersection of Johnson and Wesselman Roads. Today, this intersection is one of the busiest and fastest growing areas of Green Township. One only needs to look around as one drives down Harrison Ave. and observe the new shopping centers and condominiums being built and adding to the increased traffic flow along the once dirt and macadam Harrison Pike. This community was first known as Challensville, named after a preacher who was very well known in the area. Charles Reemelin, who owned a farm in Challensville, used his influence as a member of the state legislature to have the area renamed after a physical attribute of the area. The name Dent came from the topography of the area. Reemelin didn't like the use of people's names to name an area. The name stuck in 1846

The Dent Drive-In Theatre, was a fixture along Harrison Ave for many years. Today, the site is host to Veterans Park, one of the busier parks in the Green Township Park System with soccer & baseball fields, a party shelter, walking track, playground, and racquetball courts. (Photo Courtesy the Green Township Historical Association)

The Dent Schoolhouse served the children of this portion of Green Township for many years. After township school consolidation, the building was used as a machine shop, and later a haunted house attraction during Halloween. (Photo courtesy Green Township Historical Association)

when the name of the post office was changed to the Dent Post office. The old Dent Schoolhouse still exists today, still entertaining children and teens as a haunted house every Halloween season. The old Dent Drive-in Theatre has given way to a popular Green Township park, Veterans Park. Today, Dent is a fast growing area of the township, with many homes and businesses being built at a quickening pace; the addition of Interstate 74 interchanges being widened and streamlined, and the re-routing of Rybolt has contributed to the rapid and exciting development of the area. The addition of The Good Samaritan Medical Center, as well as a Veterans Memorial and Bell Tower add excitement to an already burgeoning area.

<u>Mack</u>

The Green Township community of Mack is located west of Bridgetown along Cleves-Louisville Pike(now Bridgetown Rd.). Its epicenter is the Five points intersection of Bridgetown Rd, Ebenezer Rd, and Taylor Rd. Until the 1880's, the area was known by many as Dry Ridge. The name was changed in 1892 when enough people lived in the area for the establishment of a post office. Because there already was a Dry Ridge in another part of Ohio, the name had to change. As the story goes, there was a dog that was well known to many people in the area that belonged to the Avery Markland family, which ran a store at the five points. The dog was a hound dog, and its name was Mack. So the people of Dry Ridge decided to rename the area Mack, after this notorius dog known to patrol the area.

The area is also the home to the Ebenezer Methodist Church, known today as Oak Hills United Methodist Church. It was established in 1839. Among its many preachers was a young teacher named Samuel Lewis. He later gained prominence as the first Superintendent of Ohio Public Schools. Mack was also a

This aerial shot of the "Five Points" intersection shows Mack in the 1940's. This area today is burgeoning with businesses and traffic. (Photo courtesy Green Township Historical Association)

very sparse community, set up to serve the needs of the farmers and their land. Blacksmiths, churches, and dry goods stores were what one would find in the 1800's and early 1900's. Today, it is an area that is very much like its other Green Township neighbors, the home to businesses such as car repair shops, gas stations, butcher shops, and barbershops and even mid and upper level income subdivisions. Much like Bridgetown, Mack has evolved into a sprawling bedroom community, teeming with life.

Monfort Heights

Monfort Heights has its epicenter at the intersection of North Bend Rd and West Fork Rd. It stretches up and along North Bend and West Fork Rd. In the 1800's this area was known as Wisenburg(or Weisenberg). The individuals who lived here were mostly German farmers who gave this area its name. In 1900, a local resident named Frank Lumler became the postmaster of a new post office on Burnt Schoolhouse Road(Cheviot Rd). He named this branch of the Post Office after the current Postmaster General of Cincinnati, E.R. Monfort, who was a Captain in the Army during the Civil War. The branch closed in 1905 and the name was almost lost until the consolidation of some of the one and two room schools in the area in the 1920's. The consolidated school was named Monfort Heights after the Monfort Post Office, and Heights for the high altitude of the area.[24] Growth remained slow in Monfort Heights, since most of the large farms proved too far out for true suburban growth until the post WWII baby boom when subdivisions, shopping centers, and cars began to replace open fields of wheat, corn and tomatoes as well as pens full of pigs, chickens, and cows. Today, this area is a bustling community of Green Township, home to many large and small businesses, a well as many large and

---

[24] Scully, 44

Monfort Heights takes its name from E.R. Monfort, a Captain in the Union Army during the Civil War, and later Postmaster General of Cincinnati. This photo shows the welcome sign which greets visitors to the area after they exit Interstate 74(Photo by Joe Flickinger)

small homes. Like its neighbor, Bridgetown, Monfort Heights has no real borders to contain it, only memories of far gone country hamlets meant to serve the needs of the farmers. Today, the major shopping areas serve this burgeoning bedroom community. In 2009, it was announced that a new Mercy Hospital was planned for construction along Boomer road close to North Bend Road. The new hospital brings a solution to a vital need in Green Township, that of a full service hospital as well as much needed jobs to the area. The future of Monfort Heights is very bright for the forseeable future.

White Oak

The community of White Oak is a bustling community in Green Township bordered by Monfort Heights to the south, and Colerain Township to the North. A portion of White Oak lies within the borders of Colerain Township as well. In pioneer times, it received its name from the abundance of White Oak trees that prospered in the area. White Oak lumber was valued for its "tight cooperage", or the fact it made great material for kegs and barrels. White Oak wood is described as being "naturally plugged" so the wood is non-porous. The original settlers in the area were predominately German immigrants, who helped play a valuable role in the 1800's beer boom in Cincinnati, where beer was one of many vital industries in the German dominated city. At first the area was named St. Jacobs, named after the St. James Catholic Church that still is situated in the area. Jacob is the German word for James. In the later 1800's the area was called Creedville after a post office that was situated at Blue Rock and Banning roads in Colerain Township. By the 1920's, the area was now called White Oak, harkening back to the first settlers who preferred the trees in the area for their trades and consumption.

Covedale

When many Green Township residents hear the name Covedale, they think of the Covedale Theatre and Library and the rest of the business district along Glenway Ave up to Cleves Warsaw inside the City of Cincinnati. They also think of the area as uniquely Cincinnati. Until 1930 most of this area was uniquely Green Township, when the City of Cincinnati annexed this portion of the township. Before this area was subdivided for homes, it was home to many dairy farms, nurseries, and a few vineyards. These areas were described as having pleasantly rolling fields with coves and dales, which gave the area its name, Covedale. Today, some of the residential portion of this area is still situated in Green Township, west of Covedale Ave., along Sidney and north of Cleves Warsaw Pike. It is also home to a newer Green Township fire station on Sylved Road, and a newly rebuilt Covedale Elementary in the Cincinnati Public School System.

Westwood

When one mentions Westwood, one thinks of the largest neighborhood in Cincinnati. With over 35,000 residents, this vibrant community has the suburban appeal, yet resonates with all the attributes of the city. Believe it or not, Westwood made up the southeastern portion of Green Township. During the 1800's, Westwood gained popularity as the place to get away from the dirt, grime, and smog of the 1800's industries that often contributed to poor health. Consequently, Westwood became home to sprawling estates, which were home to some of the most influential families of Cincinnati. The Gambles, Werks, and Oskamps were some of the families who ventured outside of the crowded city to escape the dirt and smells. In 1868, Westwood incorporated as a village becoming more of an independent entity from Green Township government, and in 1896 the village of Westwood became a neighborhood of the City of

This photo shows the Cincinnati and Westwood Railroad crossing from Westwood into Green Township over today's Glenmore Ave., towards its terminus near the Robb Farm. Notice that Glenmore Ave. is a dirt road, and there appears to be nothing in the background but open fields. (Photo courtesy Cincinnati Historical Society Library)

This photo shows the same area today. The old tracks would have crossed roughly through where the middle of the bricked building with the white sign is located. The station would have been located roughly where the driveway is located to the left of the building. The slope up of the ground is visible in the older picture. Notice how everything is now a built out urban area. (Photo by Joe Flickinger)

Cincinnati when the city annexed the village. It was Westwood that ultimately helped bring the population explosion to Green Township when the city extended its streetcar lines to Westwood. These lines replaced the Cincinnati & Westwood short line train which ran from the Robb Farm in Cheviot to the Brighton depot in downtown Cincinnati.

The History of Cheviot

Cheviot's history traces back to 1796 when a pioneer named James Smith hacked his way through the woods and discovered a large spring. He built a small cabin and even managed to clear a couple acres. But he soon left, and Jacob Johnson came in, clearing forest for what would become Harrison Pike. Cheviot was platted on land that was won by Elias Boudinot in his case against John Cleves Symmes over compensation from the Symmes Purchase. In 1818, Cheviot was platted and named by John Craig Sr., who hailed from the Scottish hills known as Cheviot that separated Scotland from England.

The Seven Mile House was one of the most well known establishments of the town, situated at the "old Forks", where Bridgetown Road and Harrison Pike meet and split. The Cheviot Tavern was also a well known establishment close to the Beech Flats Spring, found by James Smith in 1796. The Seven Mile House sat where Cheviot School is today; The Cheviot Tavern sits near where Kenker Place is today. Cheviot was governed by the Green Township Trustees until 1901, when in July of that year the incorporation of the village of Cheviot took place. Nonetheless, Cheviot contributed a number of firsts to Green Township before becoming its own village. In 1806, an open house celebration on the Enoch Carson Farm celebrating that year's abundant harvest was held. Neighbors from farms all through Green Township attended and brought food for all to enjoy. Through the years, the open house picnic evolved into a festival, which

This photo shows the Seven Mile House, located where Cheviot school is presently. This hotel was an important stop for any farmer driving his livestock from Green Township to the stockyards located in Cincinnati. (Photo Courtesy Green Township Historical Association)

The Harvest Home Fair still has many competitions and contests, including the Fruit and Vegetable competition, popular to this day. (Photo courtesy Green Township Historical Association)

in recent years included contests, exhibitions, and a parade. Today the Harvest Home Festival still boasts a parade covered by all the major media outlets, exhibitions of art, livestock, and fruits and vegetables, and of course the fair itself. Dinners and raffles and other contests and rides are for all to enjoy. Today the fair organizers boast that it is "the biggest little fair in Ohio".

Another first is what is reputed to be one of the first prize fights held in Ohio. The following is an excerpt from the *Cincinnati Daily Gazzette* from June of 1837, describing its outrage over the "organized" nature of the fight held in what was the little Green Township hamlet of Cheviot:

CINCINNATI DAILY GAZETTE - JUNE 28, 1837 ISSUE, PAGE 2

<u>OUTRAGE</u> *"A flagitious outrage upon our laws, and upon decency and humanity, was perpetrated in the vicinity of our city on Monday afternoon, June 26 [1837]. An Englishman and an Irishman, both of some recent importation we presume, appointed Cheviot their theatre for the sports of the ring. A large concourse of people gathered together; the two demi-bruts actually met and, for a bet of money (it is said $1000), beat and bruised each other shamefully. We call attention to this violation of the law. All concerned, and especially the boxers, and their associates of every description, are guilty of a riot. Let witnessed be summoned before the grand jury, and an example be made of the parties, no matter who they may be, that has countenanced by their presence and approbation, this brutal exhibition. It is the first of the kind that has disgraced our state: it is of importanceit should be branded with all the reprobation that can be heaped upon."*[25]

---

[25] "Outrage" Cincinnati Daily Gazette, June, 28, 1837 Page 2

Yet another first was the first horse track in the area, located close to what is today an area bounded by Westwood Northern Boulevard, Washington Ave. and Homelawn Ave. This area was later converted to a baseball field until Cheviot Field house was finished by the village of Cheviot in the 1930's.

Today, Cheviot is its own city, making the change from a village to a city in November, 1965 leaving Green Township.[26]

---

[26] Roger Miller, Western Hills Press, 11/18/1965 Vol. XLII No. 3 Western Hills Press Publishing

Chapter Four:
The 20th Century, and the changes it brought.

The onset of the "War to end all Wars", the car, the streetcar, and the telephone began to shrink the world as people knew it in the early 1900's. Cincinnati was enduring as a major Midwestern city. Its recovery from the Civil War was minimal- without any major battles in the Greater Cincinnati area; Cincinnati remained intact as a major city. The problems it had in the 1900's forward were corruption and stagnation. George "Boss" Cox and his political machine were doing their best to maintain control of the city and its government. In the meantime, life in Green Township continued on at its own slow pace. Cheviot was still growing, but was miniscule in physical size compared to Cincinnati. Cheviot officially declared itself a village, incorporating in 1901. Besides the eventual loss of Cheviot, Green Township lost several other parts and parcels of land to the encroachment of the City of Cincinnati. Westwood was annexed by Cincinnati in 1896. Westwood had incorporated as a village a few years back, and was now on the path to becoming one of the largest neighborhoods in the City of Cincinnati by 2009. Also, portions of Covedale, Mt. Airy, Price Hill, and another smaller portion of Westwood were annexed in the early 1900's. Still, by 1920 there were around 548 farms spread throughout Green Township. While many of these farms were 50 acres or less, they were a bountiful food source for the city of Cincinnati. Transportation issues to the farms of Green Township and recently annexed Westwood remained the issue of getting over the Mill Creek and adjacent rail yards. This was solved by the construction of the Harrison Avenue Viaduct in 1908. While this eased some of the issues, it was considered a temporary fix.

Working on the farm is Ralph Schlensker, driving a "wheat wagon". Sights like this one became less and less common after WWII in Green Township.(Photo courtesy Schlensker/Springmyer Families)

Street Cars and Railroads:

While Cincinnati enjoyed some form of horse drawn street car system since the mid 1800's, Green Township has not had the opportunities that other parts of the city have had. Green Township has been landlocked from its formation in 1809. This meant that travel could not occur from some form of major waterway. This meant that the only way in or out was by roads. The roads up to the early 1900's were not the smooth, steady, black-topped roads we all know today. The roads of Green Township since its inception were dirt, gravel, or macadam roads. The dirt roads either went to macadam, or to paved roads. Macadam roads were considered to be a combination of crushed rock and gravel. With the takeover of many of the private turnpikes by Hamilton County in the late 1800's, many were paved over by asphalt. But just because the roads were paved over, didn't mean the streetcars would come to Green Township. Lack of population, and profitability became major issues for streetcars when it came to expansion. The population of Green Township and surrounding areas hindered expansion of street cars into the area until street cars arrived in Westwood in the early 1900's. In the meantime, several initiatives were tried, but ultimately proved unsuccessful. A narrow-gauge railroad named the Cincinnati-Westwood short-line railroad was built and operated from downtown to the Westwood/Cheviot area not once, but twice. It occured first in 1874, then in 1887 it was reopened after being closed for a year. It was converted to a standard gauge railroad in 1891, and was completely abandoned in 1926 after serving freight traffic for several years because

This picture shows the No. 2 Engine of the Cincinnati-Westwood RR and its crew. From Left to Right; George Mygapp, George Johnston, Erasmus Tate, Phil Heubach. And Val Heubach in 1892. (Courtesy Cincinnati Historical Society Library)

streetcars killed passenger traffic.[27] Some of the old rightaway can be seen today if one knows what one is looking for. In its heyday, the Cincinnati & Westwood(C&W) carried 17 trips per day each way between Green Township and Cincinnati's Brighton terminal.[28] Many individuals took excursion trips to Metz's Wine Garden on Queen City Avenue, which enjoyed great success until the 18th amendment brought about the closing of the establishment. Further hampering the C & W was the establishment of street cars into Westwood in 1898. This led to its demise noted earlier, since street cars were easier to ride, more numerous, and much quicker to ride into downtown Cincinnati. The Cincinnati Street Railway Company bought the C & W's line and right away and resold it in parcels to private individuals and businesses.[29]

  The streetcars have been the slow and steady mechanism that helped to jump start the eventual growth and boom of Green Township as a residential suburb. As noted, the attempts at establishing railroads as a reliable and quick form of transportation to and from Green Township proved to be an experiment in futility. Considering the terrain in the western hills of Cincinnati, the C & W had many steep grades and sharp turns on its trek towards Green Township. The pollution from the engine car was very dirty and didn't sit well with the farmers and estate owners of the Green Township area since many liked the open, clean air of the country compared to the dirty, hazy unclean aspects of the city. When electric lines were stretched to Green Township via Westwood, it made the inevitable death of the trains and birth of the cleaner streetcar a much more viable solution. As a result, the Westwood, Cheviot, and

---

[27] Albert D. Shockley, <u>Achivement in Western Hills,</u>(Cincinnati Ohio, Westwood Civic Association, 1932) 42-43
[28] Hale,20
[29] Shockley, 43

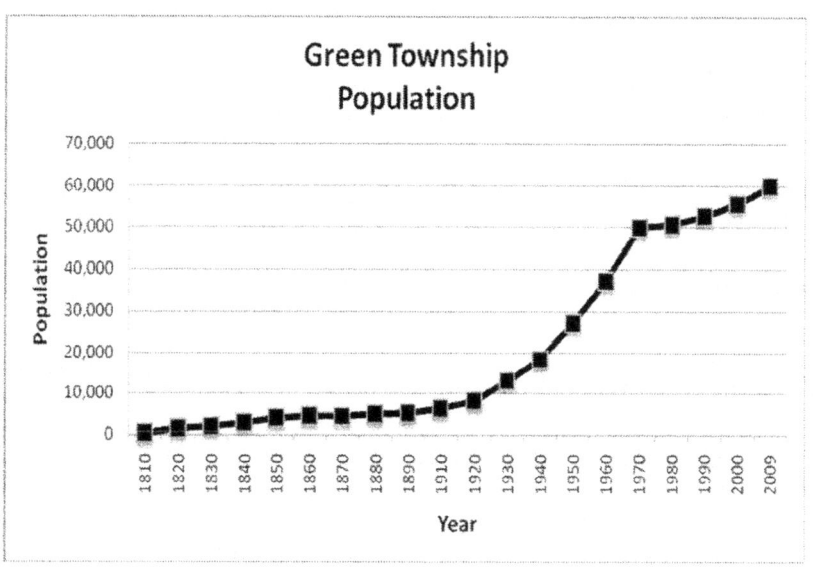

Green Townships population remained small and steady until streetcars came to the area in the early 1900's. Notice how the population skyrockets upward, especially during the baby-boom years. The 2009 data is based on a Census estimate. (Data courtesy Green Township Historical Association)

subsequently Green Township areas began to grow. In 1880, the population of Green Township stood at roughly 4800 inhabitants. The Harrison Ave. viaduct was built in 1908 making travel to the western side of the county much easier by wagon, streetcar, and one by one, a "horseless carriage" or two. By the turn of the century there were still many farms in Green Township. When even the Harrison Ave. Viaduct became overcrowded, overused, and unsafe, plans were drawn up to construct a new gateway to the western portion of the county. As part of the bonds package that built the Union Terminal Train Station, the Western Hills Viaduct was constructed and opened in 1932, all despite the Great Depression raging in our country.[30] The construction of this roadway made the travel into Green Township much easier, and as a result, the population of Green Township exploded in the years leading up to the Second World War. The street cars, the cars, and the opening of the roads that supported them brought about the slow disappearance of farms, and the gradual appearance of houses and subdivisions.

An Airport?!?

One of the surprising facts that many township residents do not know is that Green Township once had its own airport. This airport emerged in the dusk of the roaring twenties. Greater Cincinnati was experiencing a surge in smaller, regional airports besides the bigger "hub" airports such as Lunken Airfield located near the river and owned and operated by the city of Cincinnati. Colerain Township had one, located close to where the Northgate Mall is today. Green Township was no different. In 1928, around 59 acres was purchased from Judge George Eyrich, by a Dr. E.S. Simmonds. These 59

---

[30] E.W. Clark, Achievement in Western Hills(Cincinnati Ohio, Westwood Civic Association, 1932) 6-8

This is opening day from the Frank Airport.
(Photo courtesy Green Township Historical Association)

acres were located off of Cincinnati-Louisville Pike, today's Bridgetown Road. Dr. Simmonds and his partner, Harry Frank, planned on building a small airport for the slowly growing Green Township. Even though aviation was still brand new and was mostly for the well to do, many individuals turned out for the opening on August 10th, 1929. This grand opening featured the sister ship of the Spirit of St. Louis, as well as many other aircraft from surrounding airports performing stunts and flybys, as well as being displayed on the ground for all to see. The Frank Airport as it was called, was to be mainly a draw for parachuters and private flyers. Its main claim to fame is being a staging area for relief supplies during the great Ohio River flood of 1937, provoking massive devastation due to the over 80 foot flood of the Ohio River.

  The Frank Airport had a north-south runway, as well as an east-west runway. While both runways were grass, the North-South runway was used most often. The east-west runway was only used in the event of a strong cross wind event. The sad ending to the story of the Frank Airport is the story of many businesses that tried to endure during our nation's deepest and most destructive depression. While it played a major role in relief supplies during the 1937 flood, the airport was plagued by bad business. With only around 10,000 inhabitants, commercial flights to and from Green Township were non-existent, and parachuters and private planes only brought in a small percentage of the money needed to operate the airport. It's ownership changed hands several times over the 1930's resulting in a name change to the Western Hills Airport, and finally the Cheviot Airport in 1945. The final nail in the coffin for the airport was the onset of WWII, which called away

This photo shows the top of the hangar donated to the Miami University Airport by the old Frank Airport. (Photo by Joe Flickinger)

many of the pilots needed to fly, act as trainers and plane mech anics for the war effort.[31]

There are, though, some distant reminders of the airport. The curved top hanger was taken apart and moved to Miami University in Oxford Ohio where it is still located today. Also, many of the backyards of the residents of Neiheisel and Eyrich that butt up to one another are very flat. These areas comprised the north-south runway of the airport. Also, some of the older houses along Eyrich were in existence and witnessed the airplanes that flew over Green Township during the "Golden Age" of flying.

Telephones

Telephones were few and far between in Green Township. They relied on the wires on telephone poles we all know and don't pay much attention to today. But phones in Green Township in the early 1900's were a luxury, or to most, a novelty. Phones in homes were completely unheard of until 1902, when Cheviot granted an ordinance to the Cheviot, Mt. Airy, and Groesbeck Telephone company to set poles and wires for home phone service. Until that time, a telephone exchange had been established in Cheviot on the corner of Harrison Ave. and North Bend Roads. If one wished to reach someone in the township, a messenger was sent to wherever in the township the person lived, and that person was summoned to the operators phone at which point the operator called the person who originally called, and the conversation took place. If it sounds like a long process, it was! This is why to everyone, phones were a novelty in Green Township.[32] In 1906, the Cincinnati and Suburban Telephone Company (today's Cincinnati Bell) purchased the Cheviot, Mt. Airy, and Groesbeck company and all its assets, further bringing more phone poles and lines to

---

[31] Kyle Vath, <u>A History of the Frank Airport, 1928-1950</u>; Unpublished Manuscript for Eagle Scout Project.
[32] Scully, 26-27

most of the township. This didn't mean that the township enjoyed greater phone service though. Since many of the houses sat far back from the roads, the expense proved too great for hook up for a phone. As a result, the reach and ring of a phone didn't fully saturate the township until after the First World War.[33]

Electricity

From the first settlers until around 1918, the only way for people to see after the sun had gone down was by the fireplace, a torch, or kerosene or oil lamps. Needless to say, the township became very quiet after the sun went down. As mentioned in a previous chapter, a "potato hole" was one method for refrigeration of the many perishable foods such as milk or cheese. But as the township became more populated, the need for better storage became a necessity. Making preserves became a necessary component of either the wife or daily chores of the daughter. Many types of fruits and vegetables were canned or preserved in glass jars out of the basic need for food in the winter. Without a huge grocery store that brought in fresh food from all over the world, it was impossible to drive the wagon or ride a streetcar to downtown Cincinnati to the many markets selling goods for consumption every week. The roads were either impassable due to snow, ice and rain or, the streetcar ride was so long a majority of the day was spent traveling to and from town. So what many in the township resorted to was the use of ice in an icebox. Many people today hear grandparents or great-grandparents refer to the modern refrigerator as an "icebox". Before electric refrigerators and electricity became widespread in the township, many had a business that would deliver ice blocks to sit in an upper compartment of a small fridge and the ice would help keep perishables such as milk and

---

[33] Scully, 26-27

other items fresh for a few days.[34] Another way to keep food fresh would be to lower food in a basket down an unused well. Watermelon was kept this way in the summer, to be consumed around the July 4th holiday picnics. But when it came to electricity, just like the phone lines, the township was slow to be hooked up. Even though lines would be strewn all over the main roads like Harrison Pike and Bridgetown Road, many would not voluntarily get hooked up because of the cost involved. Many of the brave farmers who could afford the cost would pay $50.00 to the Cincinnati Gas, Light, and Coke Company to be hooked up to the commodity that today, we cannot seem to live without. Without the luxury of electricity, many in Green Township would cook over a wood stove, use coal-oil lamps, and go to bed and wake up in very cold rooms.[35]

Religion in the Township

Green Township has a long and storied religious tradition in the confines of the township. Today, many longtime residents look forward to the summer months, where bake sales, rummage sales, and festivals dominate the houses of worship. If a visitor were to ask a native Cincinnatian where to get a good fish sandwich during Lent, inevitably they would point the visitor to Green Township, which has a reputation as being home to many Roman Catholics. But that was not always the case. Roman Catholics were not always the dominant religion in the area.

The first church in the township was built by Enoch Carson on what became Harrison Avenue in 1811. It was built in front of the old Bethel Cemetery. Unfortunately this first church did not last long, as a tree reportedly fell on it and rendered it "beyond repair." Later, around 1824, a group of Baptists built a new

---

[34] Scully, 27-28
[35] Scully, 27-28

church of brick and logs on the same site. This first church became known as Bethel Baptist Church. It had originally been organized as the Baptist Society of Green Township in 1821 and became the Bethel Baptist Church in June of that year. The first minister of the church was George Hildreth, who served in this capacity until he passed in 1824.[36]

The Methodists also came and at first rented their church from the Presbyterians. They built their first church in 1842 in Cheviot. Their first preacher was George W. Maley.[37]

Ebenezer Methodist Church was established in the hamlet of Dry Ridge(Today's Mack) around 1839 in part due to a prominent family of merchants in the area: the Marklands. One of their early preachers was a young Samuel Lewis, the future first Superintendent of Ohio's Public Schools. Their first permanent building was built of brick in 1849, but was unfortunately destroyed by a tornado in 1866. It was rebuilt almost immediately, a feat that was unheard of for the 1800's. Amelia Wilke donated some land and money for a new church in 1940, as a memorial to her late husband. Wilke Memorial Church functioned until 1967, when their name changed to Oak Hills United Methodist Church and in 1971 they built their current sanctuary and fellowship hall.[38]

The Presbyterians also arrived very early to Green Township. By 1827, services were held in many log cabins of the group's members, until 1840 when they built a brick church in Cheviot. One of their early preachers was Dr. Kendall.[39]

---

[36] Hale, 17
[37] Hale, 17
[38] Jeff Lueders, Hamilton County's Green Township(Chicago, Illinois, Arcadia Press, 2006) 95
[39] Hale, 18

Yet another old congregation is the Pilgrim United Church of Christ. Its roots go back to 1870, when a group of 43 "liberal" Protestants broke off from another congregation and met at Dr. G.H. Musekamps house to form the First German Protestant Church. The First German Protestant Cemetery donated a half acre to the congregation for their first building on Cleves Pike, now Bridgetown Road. The church building served the congregation for 90 years until a new building was built. This new building was built from 1961-62, and dedicated in 1963. Its steeple still houses the original bell which was cast at the Buckeye Foundry in Cincinnati Ohio.[40]

Roman Catholics, though, were few and far between in Green Township in the early days of our township. A small trickle of Catholic settlers began moving into the area with the influx of Southern German and Austrian settlers to the Cincinnati area in the immigration booms of the mid 1800's. The Roman Catholic Church began making inroads into the predominantly Protestant Cincinnati with the formation of the Cincinnati Diocese in 1821 with Bishop Edward Fenwick as the first Bishop.[41] This led to many German Catholics settling in Cincinnati. The "mother" church of Roman Catholics in Green Township was St. Jacobs, which later was renamed St. James the Greater.

St. James was established in 1840, with the first mass being held in the Oehler barn. The first log cabin church was built in 1841 at a cost of $124.62. The formal establishment of the parish has been set as 1843. The church currently serves around 2300 families, and serves a mostly suburban worshipper. Many of the churches that were later established in Mt. Healthy, Taylor Creek,

---

[40] Leuders, Jeffrey, <u>Pilgrim United Church of Christ, 1870-1990</u>(Church Printing, 1990)

[41] Roger Fortin, <u>Faith and Action, A History of the Cathoilc Archdiocese of Cincinnati, 1821-1996</u>(Columbus Ohio, The Ohio State University Press, 2002) 11

This picture shows the First German Protestant Church that was built on Cleves Pike(Bridgetown Rd) in 1871. This building lasted 90 years until the congregation changed its name to Pilgrim United Church of Christ, and built a bigger complex on the same spot with a church, offices, and fellowship hall. (Photo courtesy Pilgrim United Church of Christ)

Photograph of one of the earlier buildings of the Ebenezer Methodist Church, currently called the Oak Hills United Methodist Church. (Photo courtesy Green Township Historical Association)

and Dry Ridge have been established in the former territory of St. James.

The 2nd oldest Catholic Church in Green Township is St. Aloysius Gonzaga, established in 1866, with a brick church being built in 1867. St. Aloysius, much like St. James, outgrew several church buildings. St. Aloysius built its current church in 1963. Today, St. Aloysius' territory is much smaller, having given way to the establishment of the Catholic Parishes of St. Catherine(1903), St. Martin Of Tours(1911), Our Lady Of Lourdes(1927), St. Ignatius(1946), Our Lady of Visitation(1947), and St. Jude(1956) Catholic Churches.[42]

Cemeteries

The first cemetery in Green Township is the Cemetery located in the heart of Cheviot on Harrison Ave. near Glenmore. It was established on January 15, 1822. It was originally located on both the north and south sides of Harrison Pike. The South side of the cemetery later was renamed the Green Township cemetery. These cemeteries were active during the 1800's. The 1900's, and its population spike in the area meant people were going to other cemeteries due to lack of space. The Bethel Cemetery is currently attended to by the City of Cheviot. The Green Township Cemetery was moved to Bridgetown Cemetery in 1976.
The St. James and St. Aloysius Catholic Churches each have their own cemeteries. The St. James cemetery was established in 1843, and is still active today. The St. Aloysius Gonzaga cemetery was started in 1868, and is still active today as well. Both of these cemeteries have served their parishes well, and are the last resting place of many of the original parishioners of these two early Catholic churches in the township.

The biggest, and still very active cemetery in the township today is the Bridgetown Cemetery. Originally,

---

[42] Fortin, 397-398

One of the early buildings for St. James in White Oak. (From St. James Centenary Jubilee 100th Anniversary Booklet 1843-1943)

St. Aloysius Gonzaga's first church (on the right) and second church (on the left), as well as the small priest rectory (in the center). These two churches were replaced by 1963 by the third church built by the parish. (picture courtesy Green Township Historical Association

the cemetery was established in December of 1864, during the waning months of the Civil War. It was established as the First German Protestant Cemetery. Many of the German Protestant inhabitants of Green Township wanted a cemetery closer to the farms and geographic center of the township. Besides that, the Bethel and Green Township cemeteries in Cheviot were small, and it was becoming increasingly clear that both of these cemeteries would not be able to accommodate the influx of inhabitants for the township. Originally the Bridgetown Cemetery was comprised of 7 ½ acres along Cleves-Louisville Pike(today's Bridgetown Road), and would later donate 1 ½ acres to the First German Protestant Church for their first Church building (today's Pilgrim United Church of Christ). In 1876, the trustees of the cemetery hired a local stone mason, Phillip Steinman, to build a receiving vault. It was to be used for the storing of bodies until the services were ready to be held. It could also act as a safe place to guard against grave robbers stealing bodies to sell to the medical schools in the city. The receiving vault was completed, dedicated, and put into use in 1877. The Vault ceased to be used for storing bodies after the end of WWI. It is still used today as it has been since 1918- as a place to store extra equipment and tools. The original bell still resides in the steeple, and the original heavy steel doors still give an aura of a bygone era of craftsmanship not common in modern years. The vault harkens back to a time long since past, and acts as the centerpiece of the older section of the cemetery.

  Due to the increased growth in the area and the subsequent deaths, the board of trustees who oversaw the cemetery saw a need for a larger cemetery. In 1939, the cemetery bought 12.2 acres of adjacent land from the Schapkerklaus family. In 1961, the cemetery dedicated its new portion of burial grounds with speeches, singers, and prayers. In late 1963, a tributary creek of the Muddy

This photo shows the only known image of the Green Township Cemetery, which was located on Harrison Ave. across from the Bethel Baptist Cemetery. This cemetery was moved to the Bridgetown Cemetery in 1976. (Photo courtesy Green Township Historical Association)

Creek which cut the older sections and newly opened sections in half was enclosed by sewer pipe and covered over by dirt excavated from the widening of Glenway Ave. This made accessing the older section and newer sections very easy since flooding almost never occurred on a road which went over a gently rolling knoll of grass. Also in October of the same year, the cemetery's current administration building was built, providing a shop area as well as an office. In 1976, the City of Cheviot disinterred the graves of the Green Township Cemetery and had them reinterred in the Bridgetown Cemetery. A single stone was erected which pays tribute to the pioneers of the Green Township who were buried in the cemetery.[43] Today, the Bridgetown Cemetery is 19 acres of gently rolling hills, fields, and beautifully maintained gardens. It is the largest active cemetery in Green Township.

---

[43] Joe Flickinger, A History of Bridgetown Cemetery, Unpublished Manuscript, 2001

The receiving vault in the original portion of the Bridgetown Cemetery. (Photo courtesy Joe Flickinger)

This picture shows the Bridgetown Cemetery and its newer sections in 1963 as seen from the original sections. The tributary creek of the Muddy Creek that cut the cemetery in half had just been covered up with fill from the widening of Glenway Ave. (Photo courtesy Bridgetown Cemetery Association)

Chapter Five:
Post War Growth: Farms give way to Subdivisions

The major historical events of WWI and WWII brought about the sad sight of sons, brothers, husbands and fathers going off to war. Green Township played its part by sending many of its sons to fight in a war halfway around the world. WWI gave way to the 1920', and life stayed the same in Green Township, save the occasional horseless carriage or two bounding down the gravel roads. The population of the township was recovering very well from the loss of Westwood to Cincinnati. Population numbers steadily increased, especially with the establishment of streetcar lines in to Westwood and Cheviot and the increasing affordability of automobiles. This made commuting to Cincinnati an easier task. During the 1930's, Green Township joined the rest of the country in making it through the Great Depression. Economic growth slowed tremendously, and leaving the township to find a job in the city became a very attractive opportunity for second jobs. As WWII started, residents learned how to ration goods and sent their sons and husbands to Union Terminal to depart in trains to fight the Germans and Japanese. There was one constant- the rural way of life. Green Township experienced growth, but only a few houses at a time. But the entire character of the township was about to change. Shortly after the end of WWII, the GI's returning home would need housing provided from loans through the GI Bill. Many GI's did not want the noisy, dirty, and often crime prone city neighborhoods to serve as the home for their new families. In the late 1940's the Baby Boom hit and as a result, the areas once known as farming communities became prime targets for developers to build huge subdivisions to house the growing population. Green Township's population swelled as a result of the subdivisions which would permanently change the face of the township forever. Huge farms became new neighborhoods with small, cookie-cutter cape cods with 2-

3 bedrooms, a one car garage and a fenced in backyard. The area's farms slowly began to disappear. A new baby boom meant more cars, more kids, and as a result better roads, and better schools.

Fire Protection

Prior to 1954, all of Green Township was protected by five Fire Departments. These five departments covered portions of Green Township in addition to its own areas. These five departments were the Mack Volunteer Fire Department, Cheviot, Delhi, Miamitown and Groesbeck Departments. In 1954 with a growing population as well as the increased cost of runs, the township decided to enter into a contract with Mack Fire for the protection of the township. The Mack Fire Department then subcontracted with the Delhi Fire Department for the protection of the extreme southern portion of Green Township. Their original coverage area was canvassed by all of the original members of the organization, going door to door asking for donations for equipment and further buildings. Property was later purchased at the intersection of Bridgetown, Ebenezer, and Taylor roads, and a two bay garage was built to house the new pumper that was purchased, as well as an ambulance. Later, it was expanded to include a 4 bay garage, as well as a basement meeting room. All of the labor was done by volunteer union bricklayers, who worked on Saturdays for beer and food!

In the 1960's, the northeast portion of the township was growing at a fast rate, and land was purchased from the Udry Family. In 1967, the West Fork station opened, with enough room for four firefighters, a pumper, and ambulance. In 1974, the fire department added paramedic service to its list of services. Now the department could begin stabilizing a patient before getting to a hospital. Also, 1974 was a special time in the fire department's history. The first piece of

The old firehouse built with volunteer labor at the intersection of Bridgetown, Ebenezer, and Taylor Roads. (Photo courtesy Green Township Historical Association)

equipment was purchased with a township fire levy. From now on, the township would purchase any and all necessary equipment for the use of firefighters and paramedics. In May of 1977, the township built a firehouse at the intersection of Muddy Creek and Sylved Roads. It would serve the extreme southern portion of the township which included Covedale. This station was dedicated to Captain George Zorick, who was a Mack firefighter who died in the Beverly Hills Supper club fire. In the late 1970's, the township was beginning to experience the same issues and problems that many other urban areas were experiencing. This applied to available manpower for volunteer firefighters. As a result, the Mack Fire Department began to make plans to convert to a full time, professional fire department. In 1980, Robert Weitzel was named the first full time chief of the Mack Fire Department. Later that year, seven full time firefighters manned the three stations in the township. That number was increased by two late in 1980 to bring the total to nine. The overnight shift was still manned by volunteers. In 1983, the township approached the Mack Fire organization about assuming control of the department. The township was pouring more than $1 million dollars into the department with little say to how it was spent. As a result, the Mack Fire Department voted to disband, and the Green Township/Mack Fire Department was formed. Mack Fire lived on though, as Mack Fire Incorporated, a civic organization whose sole purpose was to provide social and financial support to the Fire Department. Green Township agreed to rent the Monfort Heights and Mack stations from the organization. In 1984, with the passage of another fire levy, the township replaced volunteer firefighters with part-time firefighters who worked 12 hour days. In 1992, the township fire department moved into its fourth station, located at the brand new township administration center on Harrison Ave.[44](Internet Archive, Dietz, 1998) In 2001, the township closed the original Mack Fire building at the Five Points intersection and built a brand new station just down the road at the corner of Eyrich and Bridgetown Road. It currently houses 5 firefighters 24 hours a day and services the busy Bridgetown and Mack areas, including the Glenway Avenue business district. In 2005, the Township rebuilt the Monfort Heights station #55 enabling it to house one pumper, one ambulance, and one truck with a hazardous materials trailer, as well as up to seven firefighters. This station serves the busiest section of Green Township in terms of population and calls.[45]

Police Protection

Police protection in Green Township from its founding until the mid 1800's was very sporadic. Hamilton County Sherriff deputies very rarely patrolled the outer areas like Green Township. Many townships either did not have the money or the manpower to incorporate their own police forces. Green Township was no different. So, as some livestock thefts began to increase, a group of township residents created the 77 member Green Township Anti-Thieving Association in 1885. It usually met at Fockes Tavern at Bridgetown Rd. and Church Lane. Its members took it upon themselves to search for and possibly apprehend suspects who were accused of farm crimes in the community, especially horse thieves. If a crime occurred, members spread word to the residents of the township and blocked roads while

---

[44] Tom Dietz, History Of Green Township/Mack Fire Department, 1/23/1998, Internet Archive
http://web.archive.org/web/20001204193100/www.greentwp.org/fdhx/sld001.htm; Accessed 10/20/2009

[45] Green Township Webpage, http://www.greentwp.org; Accessed 10/12/2010

This badge was used by the Green Township Anti-Thieving Association during the late 1800's when county deputies rarely ventured into unincorporated areas like Green Township except to serve court papers. The association later became a social club when county deputy patrols became more regular in the 1900's. (Picture courtesy Green Township Historical Assciation)

sometimes armed, looking for the suspect.[46] Later in the early 1900's as county sheriff protection became more widespread, the group became more of a social club.

As the county sheriff's office became more comprehensive with its protection, the anti-thieving association and others like it began to fade into the background. In all of Ohio's 88 counties, the sheriff is the chief law enforcement officer. The main duties are to provide court services and corrections on a countywide basis, and police protection to the unincorporated areas of the county. However, full police jurisdiction is maintained in all municipalities, townships and villages. Ohio sheriffs and deputies have worn a standard uniform since 1960. All vehicles are marked in the same manner.[47]

Green Township Police were established in 1959. For a time, there was no chief of police, only a Chief Constable. According to an article in the Western Hills Press, the first Chief Constable was Ralph Bender, appointed in 1965.[48] Chief Bender also was the first township constable in July of 1959. The cruiser patrol was launched in July of 1961 with three members. The First Chief of Police commissioned was Arthur Pfaff, in 1973.[49] Green Township today has 31 sworn officers, along with 13 sheriff's deputies provided by the county. The police department made over 33,000 calls, as well as over 2,500 arrests in 2008. Today it is a full service department, serving the population of Green Township 24 hours a day, seven days a week. In addition to patrol and investigations, the department also provides motorcycle patrol, bicycle patrol, crime patrol services, D.A.R.E,

---

[46] Roger Miller, "Townships Anti-Thieves Active Since '85" Western Hills Press, July 3, 1959

[47] The Greater Cincinnati Police Historical Society Museum website, Hamilton County Sherrifs Office History, Accessed 6/29/2010, http://www.gcphs.com/history.html

[48] Western Hills Press, July 1, 1961

[49] Scully, 20

neighborhood watch, Citizens Police Academy, and the LEAD tip phone line.[50]

Schools:

Green Townships schools have their roots in the old log cabins and one room school houses that one imagines from stories about pioneer education. Today's educational trends of mega schools which resemble malls or office buildings rather than the one or two room schools of yesterday would amaze our first settlers. These early pioneers were so far removed from the City of Cincinnati and its opportunities that they could never have imagined the need or cost involved with running the major school districts that Green Township supports. They would also be amazed by the vast number of residents that also choose to send their children to the many choices for private schools within the township as well. Today, Green Township is the home to three of the biggest school districts in Hamilton County. Oak Hills, Northwest, and Cincinnati Public Schools all draw from Green Township's population. There are also a number of private and parochial schools which call Green Township home as well.

It was ordered in the Congress of 1785 that every divided section or township in the Northwest Territory should have a portion cordoned off for public education. It was reaffirmed in the Ordinance of 1787.[51] It was later ordered that a section 16 in every Township had to be set aside for public education. School Section Road currently sits close to the section of land that originally was to be set aside for public education. This land was eventually sold off to private citizens for the raising of money for the "common school" as they were becoming known, where

---

[50] Green Township Website, www.greenwp.org/aboutthepolicedepartment; accessed 9/19/2009
[51] Wm G.W. Lewis, <u>A Biography of Samuel Lewis, First Superintendant of Common Schools for the State of Ohio</u>(Cincinnati,Ohio, Methodist Book Concern Publishers, R.P. Thomson Printers 1857) 98

the schools could be built elsewhere in the township if they so desired by a majority public vote.[52]

Green Township schools began in the one room buildings common in Hamilton County in the early 1800's. Only those students who could afford to go by subscription were going to an early township school. This practice was very common in many farming communities. Often, students would learn the basics; reading writing and math from a family member or neighbor. Often this was all that was needed to run a frontier farm. Those that could go to subscription schools were often few and far between. The earliest known school in the area was a log cabin school operated close to the current cemetery in Cheviot, the Bethel Baptist Cemetery, which was four acres donated by Enoch Carson, and his son, Enoch Jr., taught school there.[53] Many schools lasted only a few months, or maybe a year or two, as subscriptions and students waned with the seasons. It wasn't until a law passed in 1821 by the Ohio General Assembly that provided for the creation of school districts, school boards, and local taxation for school purposes that anything began to happen in Ohio, much less Green Township with public education for all.[54] The very first grammar and high schools in Hamilton County that were considered "common" were Woodward Grammar and High School situated just north of the old courthouse in Cincinnati. Even though taxes were not paid by citizens for the school, the fees were paid by William Woodward, a wealthy Cincinnatian who was a big supporter of common education. This venture proved very successful and provided a preview of the successes to come in public common schooling.[55] Meanwhile, in Green Township, educational life went by slowly. State mandates were

---

[52] Lewis, 104
[53] Hale, 7
[54] Lewis, 100
[55] Lewis, 107-108

slow to reach frontier areas such as Green Township and as a result, public schools like Woodward were nonexistent. There were, however, small one and two room schools built in the aforementioned districts set up with the passage of the 1821 law. There were at least 12 districts set up in Green Township when there were enough students to warrant hiring a teacher. District #1 was the Westwood district, and was later absorbed into the Cincinnati Public Schools after Westwood was annexed by Cincinnati. Cheviot was served by District #5, and later joined up with Cincinnati Public schools just as Westwood District #1.[56] There were other "smaller" district schools set up as well, including South Avenue District(#2) located today where Werk and South Roads intersect, as well as South Taylor Creek School District (#3) which was located on Taylor Road between Rybolt and Powner Roads.[57] Jessup Rd School District #6 was located on Jessup Rd, District #8 was located on the north end of what is now Interstate 74 interchange on North Bend Road, and District #11 was located along West Fork Road. All three schools were later consolidated to form Monfort Heights Elementary school district in 1930 when the residents of the north end of Green Township wished to combine their rural districts into a larger school to meet the demands of their growing population. After years of legal wrangling, the Hamilton County Prosecutor intervened and ordered the Hamilton County Board of Education to set aside the area as its own special school district, exempt from the rules of the old township system. In 1930, the new Monfort Heights Elementary School was opened and dedicated in October of that year. In the early 1950's, the people of Monfort Heights refused to merge with Green and Delhi Townships to form the

---

[56] Lueders, 69
[57] Lueders, 69-70

This picture shows the Dent School House after it was built in 1894. Another part of the school would be built onto the building's left side, making it a wider building with the bell tower in the middle of the building. (photo courtesy Green Township Historical Association)

Oak Hills Local School District, and began talks with Colerain Consolidated Schools. In March 1960, the Monfort Heights district merged with Colerain District and the new, larger district was renamed the Northwest Local District.[58]

District # 12 served the Dent area and surrounding regions. The school had been around since at least 1869, when it showed up on an 1869 map of Green Township. It served not only as an elementary school, but as a three year high school, serving grades 9-11. If a student wished to go on to his/her 12th grade year, which was a must for entrance into some colleges at the time, the Green Township School Board would pay for that student to attend other community high schools including Hughes, Taylor, or Western High School.[59] The building that everyone knows and relates to the Dent School is located today on Harrison Ave. Today it is used as a haunted house that is very popular in September and October during the Halloween season. This building dates to 1894, and after the Dent district #12 was merged with the South Avenue #2 district to form Springmeyer School in 1950, it was used as a Machine Shop and then a Haunted House.[60]

District #7 School was located at Harrison and Sheed Road. It was closed in 1930, and its students attended the Dent School. The old building which housed the school was recently torn down.[61]

The most well known district today is the old Number 4 district, which served the children of Bridgetown. The earliest known school which served Bridgetown was located at the corner of Race Road and Marie Avenue. It was established in 1864. In 1876, a new building was built across the street on the current

---

[58] Scully, 8-9
[59] Scully, 11
[60] Lueders, 84-85
[61] Lueders, 78-79

This photo shows the Bridgetown School as it looked in 1902. This location is the current home of the Bridgetown Church of Christ. (photo courtesy Green Township Historical Association)

This photo shows Race Road in the 1920's. The white building behind the car is the original Bridgetown school, which abutted Marie Ave. Across the street is where the current Bridgetown Middle School is located. The original school was later used as a private residence, and later torn down to make way for a parking lot for a local restaurant. (photo courtesy Hamilton County Engineers Office)

site of Bridgetown Church of Christ. In 1889, Bridgetown was granted the status of a Special School District, making it independent of the Township Schools. In 1940, a new building was built on its present location just north of the old building.[62] The current building has had additions built in numerous years and is currently named Bridgetown Middle School, home of the Bobcats!

The last township school is District #10. This served the children of Covedale. Todays Covedale Elementary school is roughly located close to the old number 10 schools location on Sidney Road. The current Covedale elementary school is a traditional Elementary School serving students in grades kindergarten through eighth grades, and is a part of the Cincinnati City School System, currently the third largest in the State of Ohio. Recently, Covedale Elementary was rebuilt into a state of the art building using funds from a recently passed bond issue in the City of Cincinnati.

Of the modern districts which Green Township students attend, a majority of the townships children attend Oak Hills Local School District. The Oak Hills District is a modern consolidation of the Bridgetown, Delhi, and Springmyer elementary districts, which was prompted by the Hamilton County Board of Education in April of 1956. Monfort Heights was invited to join Oak Hills as well, but the citizens of Monfort Heights/White Oak decided not to join the consolidation and joined with Colerain Consolidated schools instead. Students who wanted to attend high school went to Taylor High School in North Bend, and then to Western Hills High School until Oak Hills High School opened in 1959.

Shortly after the High School opened in 1959, it had to be expanded due to the demands of an increasing student population. In 1965, an addition was built onto the High School bringing the number of classrooms to 65.

---

[62] Lueders, 72

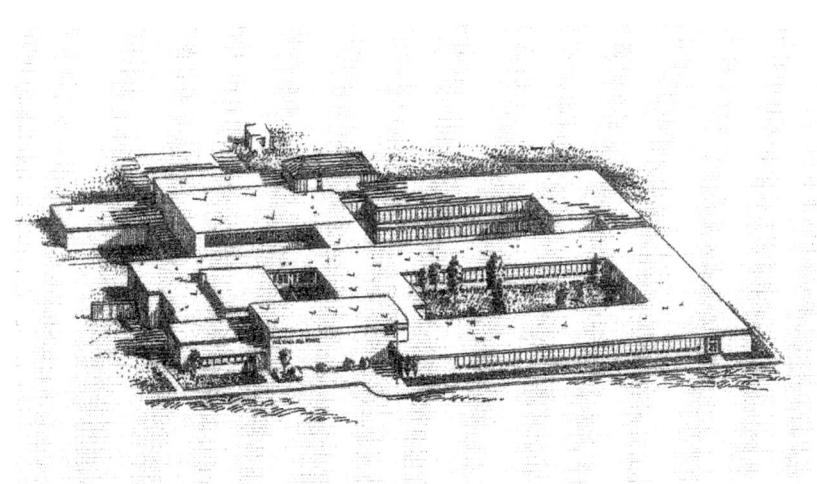

This sketch of Oak Hills High School shows the building as it looked from a 1965 addition to the passage of the 1996 Bond Issue when taxpayers approved a massive addition which enabled the district to move its freshmen to the High School campus.

Also included in this addition were a lecture room, music rooms, a gymnasium, swimming pool, auditorium, library, cafeteria, teacher's cafeteria and lounge, offices, and storage.

      Green Township's building boom in the 1980's and 1990's necessitated an addition to the crowded conditions in the high school. A bond issue was passed in November 1996, allowing the school district to enlarge the high school to accommodate the expanding population of Green Township. Today, Oak Hills High School serves almost 3,000 students from Green and Delhi Townships, making it one of largest high schools in the State of Ohio. Oak Hills Local School District is currently the third largest school district in Hamilton County, with a total student population of over 8,000 students.

Chapter Six:
Looking ahead to 200 more years

As township residents look back over 200 years of growth, modernization, and change, the next 200 years should be very exciting. The township is poised to enter into its next 200 years with much hope, promise, and potential but not without its challenges.

The year 2009 marked a momentous year for the township. Celebrations were planned and enacted for the township bicentennial. The township, led by its Bicentennial Committee, held many events. There were of course several lectures given by the Township Historical Association. These were well attended, and proved a popular attraction wherever they were held. The annual concerts held every summer at Kuliga Park were dedicated to the Bicentennial, and proved once gain to be a hit, especially the 4th of July concert and Fireworks. The Township had its first ever Kidsfest held at Veterans Park, and also had its first ever family Winterfest event held during December. The State of Ohio's first Veterans Tribute Bell Tower was built, and the bell poured on site in October. Also, the Schott Foundation provided a monetary gift to the township for the rehabilitation of the Peter Diehl house which adjoins the new Bicentennial Park on Diehl Road. This new park will host many baseball and soccer games, as well as a new Bicentennial Plaza which will hold ceremonial bricks purchased by the residents of the township.

The growth of the township is also something to look forward to as well. The announcement of the planned construction of two new hospitals in Green Township is a result of the sustained growth the Township has experienced. Mercy and Good Samaritan Hospitals both plan large facilities to be built within the township after 2009. Improved interstate entrances and exits are planned to be finished off of Interstate 74 to ease traffic concerns at both the Rybolt Exit in Dent, as well as the North Bend on ramp in Monfort Heights.

New housing and street rehabilitations occur every week, as well as the addition of a new park off of North Bend road in Monfort Heights will add to the already livable conditions in Green Township.

One looming issue the township will need to tackle will be the aging housing stock in the older subdivisions of the township. The older housing takes money to keep the structures up to standards enjoyed by the newer housing. Making sure the residents are able to keep their housing in good condition has been the goal of some new ideas like a maintenance code which was enacted in the early 2000's. These new codes were meant to help identify and help maintain what would have become nuisance properties.

Another issue which will need to be addressed is the idea of keeping the township a "livable" suburb of Cincinnati which continues to attract young families. In the early 2000's exurbs such as Mason, West Chester, and Little Miami grew from literally a farming community to a major exurban part of the Greater Cincinnati area. These areas created a great population drain on Hamilton County, and many individuals left many areas of the county in order to pursue the wide open spaces and low taxes of areas which were still run as if they were farming communities. Green Township will need to keep improving its roads in regards to congestion, its sewers in order to keep up with demand, and parks and recreation to keep the residents of Green Township secure in knowing that their recreational needs were being met right in their own area.

A final challenge the township must meet is keeping its neighborhoods and business districts from deteriorating from the loss of population, housing, and businesses moving elsewhere. The township has begun that process by enacting "self rule", in which the township has more power to create tax districts, as well as enforce more rules and regulations to make sure the community enjoys all the benefits it possibly can from a healthy, thriving area.

In the meantime though, various businesses seem to be growing and thriving in the township. Besides the hospitals and other medical offices being planned, many businesses are flourishing. Businesses such as Bridgetown Finer Meats, which harkens back to a time when meat markets and butchers were more common seems to be growing and producing high quality products. The expansion of the business into natural extensions of the meat products such as fruits and vegetables, and wines indicates the necessity to meet the fine tastes of township residents. Still other meat markets, such as Wasslers, have since moved their headquarters to Green Township in an effort to take advantage of the large population to sell their products. Other smaller stores, like Hattings grocery store, Aromas Gelato, Zip Dip Creamy Whip, and Busters Creamy Whip bring a tasty smile to the faces of the people of the township. Still larger chains seem to be targeting Green Township with newer business developments along Glenway Ave, Harrison Ave, and North Bend Rd. A new development on Glenway Ave has replaced the since closed Cronin Dodge Car dealership. It includes a Chipotle, a Chick Fil-A, and a City Barbeque restaurant. Harrison Ave is seeing a whole new slate of newer buildings and developments from Bridgetown to Dent, increasing traffic flow and patrons to an already busy business corridor. And finally North Bend Rd is seeing newer restaurants and businesses moving to this business district in anticipation of the new Mercy Hospital being built on North Bend road near Boomer Rd.

Still other businesses are proving their business practices are standing the test of time. Neidhard-Minges Funeral Home is one of those businesses. The funeral home began in 1860 in the home of Andrew Neidhard on Harrison Ave along Taylor Creek. The funeral home celebrated its 150th anniversary serving the people of Green Township in 2010, with five generations of the family working at the business.

The next 200 years will bring much change. What will the men and women of the area say about Green Township in the next 100, and then 200 years in the future?

Bridgetown Finer Meats, established in 1978, continues the tradition of quality service combined with community involvement. The business is located close to the intersection of Bridgetown Rd, Ebenezer Rd., and Taylor Rd. (Photo courtesy Bridgetown Finer Meats)

This vacant piece of real estate located along Boomer and North Bend Roads is slated to be the future home of a Mercy Franciscan Hospital. This will give township residents a full care hospital close to home without need for travel to Clifton or other parts of the city for full hospital care. (Photo by Joe Flickinger)

This log cabin, located at West Fork Park on West Fork Road, houses the German Heritage Museum. It had a previous life as a cabin built by the Feist Family in nearby Delhi Township around 1840. The family donated the cabin to the German American Citizens League for a planned museum. Today, the cabin hosts the museum, as well as acts as a cultural attraction commemorating the contributions of German immigrants and their families to the Greater Cincinnati area. (Photo by Joe Flickinger)

The Good Samaritan Hospital at Western Ridge Medical Center was opened in late 2010. It is located in the growing Harrison Ave. corridor in Taylor Creek. It includes doctors' offices, outpatient services, and an emergency room. The northern portion of Green Township can now rely on close by medical care in a growing portion of the community. (Photo by Joe Flickinger)

The Good Samaritan Hospital at Western Ridge Medical Center was opened in late 2010. It is located in the growing Harrison Ave. corridor in Taylor Creek. It includes doctors' offices, outpatient services, and an emergency room. The northern portion of Green Township can now rely on close by medical care in a growing portion of the community. (Photo by Joe Flickinger)

Appendix 1

Green Township Names Then and Now

Then	Now
Beech Flats	Cheviot
Weisenburg	Monfort Heights/White Oak
Dry Ridge	Mack
St. Jacobs	White Oak
Challensville	Dent
Burnt Schoolhouse Rd.	Cheviot Rd.
Pleasant Ridge Rd.	West Fork Rd.
Cleves Pike	Bridgetown Rd.
Giffin Rd/Lincoln Ave.	Jessup Rd.
Crookshank Pike	Glenmore Rd.
Swein Rd.	Diehl Rd.
Snyder Rd.	Kleeman Rd.
Catt Rd.	School Section Rd.
Bridgetown Rd.	Glenway Ave.
Muddy Creek Pike	Sidney Rd.

Appendix 2

District #3 South Taylor Creek School Report from Alexander Long, Teacher, for Quarter Ending July 27, 1848

Number of students: 49

Males: 23

Females: 26

Average daily attendance: 23

Subjects taught: Spelling, reading, writing, arithmetic, geography, English, grammar, algebra, natural philosophy, general history

Wages paid to teacher for quarter: $75.00

Paid from school fund: $51.59

Collected from parents of scholars: $23.41

No district tax was levied for the year 1848 and no repairs made to the schoolhouse

       July 27, 1848   Alexander Long, Teacher

***Alexander Long was a teacher in Green Township in the 1840's. He taught at District 2 and District 3 Schools. About 1850 he left teaching to enter the practice of law and politics. He was elected to the US House of Representatives in 1862. ** *

Bibliography

Burress, Marjorie. "What does Kuliga really mean?." *Western Hills Press* 1977, Print.

Clark, E.W.. "Western Hills Viaduct" *Achievement in Western Hills*. Compiled. Cincinnati Ohio: Westwood Civic Association, 1932. Print.

Dietz, Tom. "History of Green Township/Mack Fire Department." *Internet Archive* 1/23/1998. n. pag. *Internet Archive*. Web. 10/20/2009. <http://web.archive.org/web/20001204193100/www.greentwp.org/fdhx/sld001.htm>.

Eckert, Allen. *The Frontiersman*. Ashland, Kentucky: Jesse Stuart Foundation, 2001. 614. Print.

Flickinger, Joe. "A History of Bridgetown Cemetery." Cincinnati Ohio: Unpublished Cemetery History, 2001. Print.

Ford, Henry and Kate. *History Hamilton County Ohio*. Cleveland, Ohio: L.A. Williams & Co. Publishing, 1881. 294. Print.

Fortin, Roger. *Faith and Action; A History of the Catholic Archdiocese of Cincinnati, 1821-1996*. Columbus Ohio: The Ohio State University Press, 2002. 11,397,398. Print.

"Green Township Website." *Green Township Webpage*. Green Township Ohio, 12/2010. Web. 9/19/2009;6/2010;10/12/2010. <http://greentwp.org>.

Hale, Harry. "Kuliga, The Pretty Land; The colorful story of Green Township, Hamilton County Ohio." *Western Hills Press*. 1949: 3,7,17,18,20. Print.

"History of Hamilton County Sherrifs Office." *Greater Cincinnati Police Historical Society Museum*. N.p., n.d. Web. 6/29/2010. <http://www.gcphs.com/history.html>.

Kendall, Reese. *Pioneer Annals of Green Township*. San Jose California: 1905. Print.

Knepper, George. *The Official Ohio Lands Book*. Columbus: Auditor of the State of Ohio, 2002. 13-16. eBook.

Kramb, Edwin. *Buckeye Battlefields*. Springboro Ohio: Valhalla Press, 2003. 105-108 Print.

Lewis, Wm. G.W. *A Biography of Samuel Lewis, First Superintendant of Common Schools for the State of Ohio*. Cincinnati Ohio: Methodist Book Concern Publishers, 1857. 98,100,104,107,108,. Print.

Lueders, Jeff. *Hamilton County's Green Township*. Chicago Illinois: Arcadia Publishing, 2006. 69,70,72,78,79,84,85,95,. Print.

McCafferty, Michael. "Kuliga Meaning." Message to Joe Flickinger. 6/16/2008. E-mail.

Miller, Roger. "Townships 'Anti-Thieves' active since '85." *Western Hills Press* July 3rd, 1959, Print.

Miller, Roger. *Western Hills Press* November 18, 1965, Print.
"Outrage." *Cincinnati Daily Gazette* June 28, 1837: 2. Print.

Pilgrim United Church of Christ, 1870-1990. Compiled. Jeff Lueders. Cincinnati Ohio: Pilgrim United Church of Christ, 1990. Print.

Reemelin, Charles. *Historical Sketch of Geen Township*. Cincinnati Ohio: Robert Clarke & Co, 1882. 9,21,. Print.

Remember When...Monfort Heights. Edited. Henry Scully. Cincinnati Ohio: Monforts Heights Civic Association, 1977. Print.

Schaible, Theresa. *My Family*. Privately Published, 1945. Print.

Schockley, Albert. "A Railroad Which has passed into History" *Achievement in Western Hills*. Compiled. Cincinnati Ohio: Westwood Civic Association, 1932. Print.

Silberstein, Iola. *Cincinnati; Then and Now*. Cincinnati Ohio: League of Women Voters, 1982. 9,10. Print.

Steinman III, Philip. *Beechwood Flats*. 1st Edition. New York NY: Vantage Press, 1960. 17,21,22,. Print.

Vath, Kyle. "A History of the Frank Airport, 1928-1950." *Boy Scouts Eagle Scout Project Research*. Cincinnati Ohio: Unpublished.

Western Hills Press July 1, 1961, Print.

Index

Andawan, LJ...33
Bates, Usual...11
Boudinot, Elias...14,46
Carson, Enoch...46,64,86
Cowan, Edward...11
Cox, George...52
Craig, John...46
Denman, Mathias...4
Edgar, David...11
Eyrich, Judge George...58
Fenwick, Bishop Edward...66
Fithian Family...31
Frank, Harry...60
Gamble Family...43
Girty, Simon...5
Goudy, Hugh...7
Goudy, James...5
Goudy, Rebecca...7
Greene, Nathaniel...12,13
Hamilton, Alexander...9
Hale, Harry J...14
Harrison, William Henry...6
Hildreth, George...65
Johnson, Jacob...7,46
Lewis, Samuel...38,65
Lumler, Frank...40
Maley, George...65

Markland, Avery...38
Monfort, E.R...40,41
Oskamp Family...43
Patterson, Robert...4
Pfaff, Arthur...84
Powell, William...11
Reemelin, Charles...14,17,35
Ruebel, Christian...33
Robb Family...44,46
Schaible, Charles...20
Schaible, Theresa...20
Simmonds, Dr. E.S...58,60
Smith, James...46
St. Clair, Arthur...9
Steinman III, Phillip...22
Stites, Benjamin...4,9
Symmes, John Cleves...4,6,7,9,10,46
Symmes, Timothy...9
Thatcher, James...11
Udry Family...79
Washington, George...5,12
Werk Family...43
Wilke, Amelia...65
Woodward, William...86
Zorick, George...81

About The Author

Joe Flickinger is a lifelong resident of Green Township. He graduated in 1997 from Oak Hills High School. He graduated in 2001 from Xavier University with a Bachelor of Arts in History and a Minor in Secondary Education. He graduated in 2006 from Xavier University with a Masters in Educational Administration. He is employed as a History Teacher in Cincinnati, where he has served as an assistant Wrestling and Track coach, as well as developed and taught a History Elective covering Local Cincinnati History. He maintains memberships in the Green Township Historical Association, The National Council of History Education, as well as the American Historical Association. He also serves as a trustee for the Bridgetown Cemetery Association. He is married and has one daughter.

www.ingramcontent.com/pod-product-compliance
Lightning Source LLC
Chambersburg PA
CBHW070459090426
42735CB00012B/2612